A PRACTICAL GUIDE TO COMPUTER
COMMUNICATIONS AND NETWORKING

Second Edition

ELLIS HORWOOD SERIES IN COMPUTERS AND THEIR APPLICATIONS

Series Editor: Brian Meek, Director of the Computer Unit, Queen Elizabeth College, University of London

ELLIS HORWOOD BOOKS IN COMPUTING

A PRACTICAL GUIDE TO COMPUTER COMMUNICATIONS AND NETWORKING
Second Edition

R. J. DEASINGTON
Senior Computing Officer
University of Strathclyde
Glasgow

ELLIS HORWOOD LIMITED
Publishers · Chichester

Halsted Press: a division of
JOHN WILEY & SONS
New York · Brisbane · Chichester · Toronto

First published in 1982
Second Edition 1984 by

ELLIS HORWOOD LIMITED

Market Cross House, Cooper Street, Chichester, West Sussex, PO19 1EB, England

The publisher's colophon is reproduced from James Gillison's drawing of the ancient Market Cross, Chichester.

Distributors:

Australia, New Zealand, South-east Asia:
Jacaranda-Wiley Ltd., Jacaranda Press,
JOHN WILEY & SONS INC.,
G.P.O. Box 859, Brisbane, Queensland 40001, Australia

Canada:
JOHN WILEY & SONS CANADA LIMITED
22 Worcester Road, Rexdale, Ontario, Canada.

Europe, Africa:
JOHN WILEY & SONS LIMITED
Baffins Lane, Chichester, West Sussex, England.

North and South America and the rest of the world:
Halsted Press: a division of
JOHN WILEY & SONS
605 Third Avenue, New York, N.Y. 10016, U.S.A.

© **1984 R.J. Deasington/Ellis Horwood Limited.**

British Library Cataloguing in Publication Data
Deasington, R.J.
A practical guide to computer communication and networking – 2nd Ed. –
(Ellis Horwood series in computers and their applications).
I. Computer networks
II. Title
001.64'404   TK5105.5

ISBN 0-85312-763-8 (Ellis Horwood Limited – Library Edn.)
ISBN 0-85312-764-6 (Ellis Horwood Limited – Student Edn.)
ISBN 0-470-20078-2 (Halsted Press)

Printed in Great Britain by R.J. Acford, Chichester.

Table of Contents

To KATE

Preface

This book was written to fill a gap between Electronic Science and Computer Science. People with a purely computing background frequently have little conception of the physical mechanisms involved in data transmission. Similarly those with a background in electronics may have little idea of how to produce computer software for communications. No knowledge of electronics or communications science is assumed: however understanding of the basic operation of stored program computers is needed. After reading and understanding this book and its examples it should be possible for the reader to proceed to writing communications software and cope with the communications hardware needed to set up a link. The book is mainly concerned with wide-area communications; we describe several protocols with special emphasis on the latest international networking standards including X.25. We also explore high level protocols for use on packet switched networks. Two popular local area network systems are described, together with packet radio and satellite systems. All the topics are covered from a practical rather than theoretical viewpoint; all the communication software for the systems described having been personally implemented.

Special thanks are due to Kate for drawing the diagrams; Sheona Cameron for helpfully commenting on the draft text; Morag Barron for patiently typing from the original draft. Acknowledgement is made to International Computers Ltd. for permission to describe their protocols; Digital Equipment Corporation for permission to describe their PDP11 computer architecture, the real-time operating system RSX11M, and the help and encouragement of my friends and colleagues in Strathclyde University.

R. J. DEASINGTON
February 1982

CHAPTER 1

Basic Concepts

1.1 REASONS FOR USING COMPUTER NETWORKS

In early computer systems operation was strictly in batch mode. The data or programs were prepared off-line (that is, on simple mechanical devices such as card or tape punches) and submitted to be run at the computer operator's discretion. When operating systems were introduced, these replaced the work of the human operators in scheduling the work so that it was done in an efficient manner. The jobs to be executed would still be prepared off-line, but would be read into the filestore of the computer to be executed when the job scheduler decided. These systems were developed into 'cafeteria' systems where users place cards in a card-reader themselves and when the job has run their output is returned to a line-printer from which they can remove their own listings. This mode of operation is still quite widely used, although no operating systems are now produced which provide only these batch facilities. Because of the high cost of early computers and the fairly limited use made of them, one computer would be required to serve many users. A single central site might run the computer, with users located both at the centre and dispersed at other subsidiary sites. These distinct sites might originally have been served by sending their batches of cards by mail or by hand to the computer centre, and receiving their printed output in the same way. When operating systems began to support use by inter-active terminals, it made little difference if the terminals were locally connected or made use of the existing telex network. The telex network operates at only 10 characters per second (cps) which is rather slow for transmitting significant quantities of data. Modems were then used allowing data to be sent over ordinary telephone lines, first at 30 cps and later at speeds up to 120 cps over ordinary dial-up lines and 960 cps over leased lines.

Providing remote terminal access only solves a small part of the data communications problem. We need some method of controlling bulk data handling peripherals such as line-printers and card-readers in order to transfer large quantities of data. For economic reasons it is wasteful to connect several terminals at a single location to a remote computer by employing a separate telephone line for each when typically a human operating a terminal only sends data at 10% of the available line speed. In order to send data from several terminals down one line, or to control bulk data peripherals and correct any errors that occur in transmission, a set of rules governing who may send data in each direction on the line, and what format the data should be sent in must by for formulated. This set of rules is called a communications protocol. Although the earliest computer networks were set up to distribute an expensive resource (the central computers) to a wide community of users, it has come to be realised that this distribution is in itself useful. Organisations which started with a central computer facility and a network now tend to distribute the computing facility, but retain the network in order to be able to share information.

The main problem in computer communications as it has evolved is one of standardisation. Each manufacturer has kept up with the latest developments in communications in its own way. The introduction of remote interactive terminals, remote bulk data handling terminals and so on occurred at about the same time for each manufacturer, but each did it in a different way, partly for commercial reasons and partly out of the chauvinist fear of using outside ideas. It is obviously to manufactuer's advantage if any communications peripherals must be obtained from that company in order to conform with its particular protocols and standards.

The largest computer company, IBM, is of such importance that it's popular inventions tend to become de facto standards. IBM was the first major company to develop a complete networking strategy for the connection of terminals, bulk data peripherals and interconnecting computers. This product was called SNA (Systems Network Architecture). It consists of several protocols at various levels of complexity and hierarchy. Some companies have provided peripherals which can be used in an SNA environment, but no other mainframe manufacturers have used it as a general strategy since it is rather oriented towards IBM's view of computing and operating systems. More recently Honeywell and ICL have released similar strategies – DPA (Distributed Processing Architecture) and IPA (Information Processing Architecture) respectively.

In retrospect it must seem unlikely that computer manufacturers could ever have got together and agreed upon a single networking standard – which manufacturer would voluntarily jettison their investment in existing products to adopt the ideas of a rival? An independent organisation already existed to ensure compatibility of telephone and telegraphy equipment when used between different countries, the International Telegraph and Telephone Consultative Committee (CCITT). This body also makes recommendations for the interconnection of data networks and its 'X' series recommendations have been widely accepted as the way forward towards a unified communications system. These recommendations specify the detailed operation of public data networks, but the same systems will be used to implement private networks, to avoid duplicating existing technology.

When the effects of this move towards standardisation come to fruition we can hope to find a situation where all networked computers will be able to communicate by sending files or jobs to one another, and interactive terminal access to any machine will be simple. This totally connected network of the future will bring its own problems. The ease of connection to different machines tends to highlight the fact that various manufacturers often provide similar facilites to users in quite different ways, due to the different design philosophies involved in their operating systems. Some research has been carried out to try to insulate users of networks from this problem by interposing a small computer between the users terminal and the network. This computer recognises a small set of keywords to perform simple operations such as listing files, examining directories or running jobs and converts them to the appropriate command for the machine to which the user is presently connected. This mechanism can however never hope to cope with more complex facilities since the user interfaces to machines of the real world are too diverse. Another problem with diversity is knowing where one can obtain the facility that is required. A directory is needed listing the types of facilities available at each address in the network in terms of both software and hardware. This directory should preferably be available as a facility on the network. Where private networks are used in addition to public networks a problem arises as to how to address a destination on a different network. On different networks quite different addressing methods may be used, on some a number may be used, on the others strings of characters. To interface between two networks a 'gateway' is needed. If the addressing methods on the two networks are quite incompatible, then the gateway should act as a host on each network which is capable of making calls on the other network under the direct control of the user. A user on one network wishing to access a host machine on the other would make a call on the gateway machine, this would probably require the user to log on and give a password for security purposes. The security aspect is especially important on gateways connected to networks which charge users for resources used. A malicious user could run-up expensive bills if he obtained access to an international network which charged for access. Once the user is logged on, the gateway will provide a limited set of commands, the most important of which will enable the user to call a host on the other network. Once the call is established, the presence of the gateway should be invisible, simply performing the necessary protocol conversions. On some networks the call operation allows extra data to be sent which can be used by a gateway computer to make a call into another network.

1.2 DESCRIPTION OF A REAL NETWORK

In central Scotland the three main universities have cooperated in a network since about 1975. The initial motive was to provide easy access to a regional computing facility in Edinburgh for the users in Glasgow and Strathclyde universities. Since these sites now have computing systems of their own of significant power and variety, the network is used both to access resources in other institutions, and interconnect those within each institution. The three centres are interconnected to form a triangular network (see Fig. 1.1).

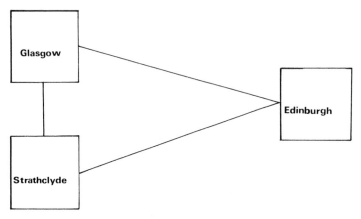

Fig. 1.1.

At each centre are special computers called 'nodes', dedicated to running the network, the various computers at each site are each connected to the local node, Fig. 1.2 shows the local connections at Strathclyde University. The mainframe computers installed at Strathclyde predate the international agreement on protocols made by CCITT and are thus connected to the regional network and the national X.25 network run by British Telecom via a PDP11/44 computer. This contains emulators for the manufacturer specific protocols of the ICL and Honeywell machines enabling them to connect to the network.

The protocol used to connect together the node processors and to connect most of the attached systems is a locally developed packet switched system called NSI. The link to the IBM 370/168 computer at Newcastle uses an IBM developed protocol termed '2780', the ICL 1904S uses an ICL protocol termed '7020', and the Honeywell 66/40 is connected using 'Remote Computer Interface' developed by Honeywell. As can be seen then, even a small part of a network of heterogeneous machines can involve the use of many protocols. It was to overcome this extravagant situation that the international standards bodies agreed on a single universal protocol — X.25. It seems probable that the universities in the UK will set up their own X.25 network based on leased lines interconnecting five main switching centres and lines from each of these nodes to the nearest universities. This would be undertaken on purely financial grounds — British Telecom charge a fixed rate per packet sent theough their network and with the volume of data transferred between universities it will be cheaper to lease lines and buy the packet switches required. Like Strathclyde's

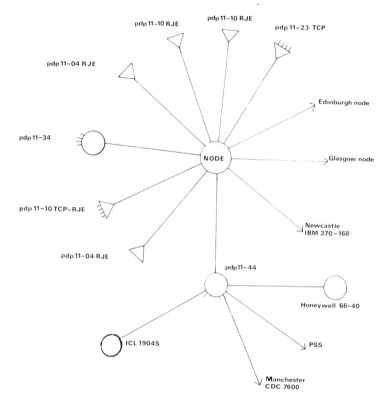

Fig. 1.2 – Connections to Strathclyde's nodes.

existing system most universities will terminate their network connection in a local node, termed a campus packet switched exchange (CPSE).

In various parts of the country there are similar networks which have evolved rather than been planned; probably most academic sites in the country are interconnected already in some obscure way but the nature of the links does not enable them to be used in a general purpose way. For example it is possible for a computer user in Edinburgh to send a file through the existing network to Strathclyde's PDP11/44, and thence to Manchester's CDC7600 machines. If the file contained the correct job control description for the CDC7600 the output from the job could be routed to a line-printer on a computer at the University of Wales Institute of Science and Technology, the reverse would also be possible. To send a file to the University of London Computer Centre (ULCC) he could route a file to Newcastle, thence to Cambridge and then on to London. To set up these obscure routes takes some considerable understanding and the access is strictly on a file by file basis, not interactive. With a unified network it should be as simple to access remote systems as it is to access local ones. The majority of interactive terminals will be connected to small computers termed 'PADs' (see 3.3.4). From a terminal connected to a PAD a simple interaction can be used to connect with equal ease to either a local machine or to a remote machine either via a private or a public network. The conversation might start by hitting the 'carriage return' character a few times so that the PAD can determine the speed at which the terminal is operating, it will then send a message of introduction. The PAD itself will have help facilities inbuilt to describe its commands, it will also contain a directory of remote computers it knows about together with a brief description of each. A 'CALL' command might be used to actually connect to a machine, for example, CALL SC6640 to connect to Strathclyde's Honeywell 66/40 computer. To access facilities through a network on which there is charging it might be necessary to provide an authorisation in the form of a username and password to identify which account should be charged and to prevent unauthorised access.

To transfer files of information or programs from one machine to another a common means will also exist with similar commands on all machines — subject to the variation in styles of command languages on different operating systems. The data will be transferred in a way such that the characters will not be transformed to others *en route*, the record sizes and boundaries will be retained and the progress of the transfer may be easily monitored. Job submission to run jobs on the various machines will also be standardised, (see 3.3.5) and life for computer users will become very much simpler through a consistent interface being available wherever they are.

1.3 SENDING DATA OVER TELEPHONE LINES

Most data transmitted to or from computers passes along telephone lines as audio signals generated by modems. We shall now attempt to explain the process of converting a digital signal in the computer, that is, one consisting only of numbers represented by binary bit patterns, to a signal suitable for the telephone system, and then converting back to digital form. These processes are called modulation and demodulation, and are carried out by a 'modem'. Historically the telephone system has been developed to optimise the transmission of human speech. Human languages contain much redundant information and send information at a fairly slow rate, hence they can withstand considerable distortion and additional noise while remaining intelligible. When digital information is being sent each piece of information has an exact meaning and any alteration to it may give it a different meaning; data, therefore is very sensitive to transmission errors which would not affect human speech. It is inevitable that errors will occur in a transmission system so higher level operations in the computer will introduce small redundancies into the message which enable the receiving computer to detect if any transmission errors have occurred and altered the values contained in the message, (see 2.5). All computer data is sent as sequences of binary digits with a value of either one or zero. Normally these binary digits are clustered into groups for use, typically into the 8 bit byte (see 2.1). For transmission over a telephone network we do not need to know about these groupings of bits or what they mean, we simply send the data bits as soon as they arrive from the data source, and regenerate them to send to the remote computer or terminal. When the computer sends out binary digits to be transmitted, they will be represented by two different electrical signal levels, for example +5V and −5V, it being specified which voltage represents binary '1' and which binary '0'. It might be thought that since most telephone circuits are terminated with four wires, two to form a transmitting circuit and two to form a receiving circuit, we could simply attach the computer interface directly to the circuit. We should then expect that if we send pulses of say +5V or −5V down it, it should emerge from the other end of the circuit as it entered, or perhaps with slight attenuation due to the resistence of the circuit. This however is not the case. To explain why it is necessary to look in more detail at the operation of the telephone system.

In early telephone systems, both the subscribers and the exhanges were interconnected by pairs of copper wires, often strung as 'open pairs' from 'telegraph poles'. To transmit over long distances by such means, amplifiers are needed to boost the signal levels at intervals. Because amplifiers are one-way devices, with distinct input and output connections, each conversation must be sent by two pairs of wires, with the amplifiers operating in opposite directions in each. Providing separate amplifiers and cable pairs for each conversation over a route is very expensive, and liable to breakdowns because of the number of devices which are needed. It was later found that radio frequency signals could be transmitted over long distances by using a specially constructed cable, called coaxial cable. If we consider the ordinary domestic radio situation we can see how this was helpful. The domestic **AM** or 'medium' waveband spans from 525 KHz to 1606 KHz and is divided (officially) into 121 channels each 9 KHz wide. We can imagine that perhaps these 121 channels might be used to provide 60 links from Glasgow to London and 60 in the reverse direction enabling 60 two-way conversations to be conducted. If instead of transmitting these 120 channels into the air with antennae we sent the signals into a coaxial cable and received them at the other end, we would have our 60 two-way conversations and still be able to use the AM waveband for domestic radio, because the coaxial cable is designed not to allow the signals it carries to leak out into space. Typically, a coaxial cable can carry a much wider range of frequencies than the AM band which is just over 1 MHz wide. The signals sent down a coaxial cable are still subject to attenuation as the distance increases but we can now use a single amplifier in each direction, designed so that it uniformly amplifies the whole range of signals the cable is carrying. This technique, called 'Frequency Division Multiplexing', and other more advanced techniques are used exclusively on the long-distance trunk networks, and increasingly on local exchange-to-exchange connections. The transmission medium is now sometimes wave-guide or fibre-optic systems, which use very high frequency radio or light respectively to carry the information, but the principle remains the same.

In using the AM waveband to describe frequency division multiplexing we mentioned that each channel allocated was 9 KHz wide, wide enough for reasonable quality music or speech, but much wider than required by telephone systems. Speech can be adequately conveyed by sending signals with a frequency of between 300 Hz and 3800 Hz, a band-width of 3500 Hz. It will be noted that the lower limit of frequency transmitted is 300 Hz, not 0 Hz (that is, a direct current) hence simply applying a constant voltage across a pair of telephone wires will not be detectable at the other end.

Having now established that the telephone system is capable of conducting electrical signals whose frequency components lie between 300 Hz and 3800 Hz, we shall now describe the mechanism by which signals can be sent over such channels by using modulated audio frequency tones. The term 'modulation' implies some change being imposed on the audio signal to transmit information. The tone which is to be modulated must have a frequency within the range of frequencies passed by the telephone system, and must be of a level so as not to overload the system and cause distortion, or be so weak that the background noise (which will always be present) interferes with it. The audio tone which will be modulated is termed the carrier. There are three possible parameters which can be altered: amplitude; frequency; and phase. In amplitude modulation the binary message being transmitted causes the level or amplitude of the carrier to be altered: when a binary zero is sent, the level of the carrier might be reduced to 0.3 of the level when a binary one is sent − see Fig. 1.3. This type of modulation is rather prone to the effects of noise, which often takes the form of short impulses. These impulses might only sound as a brief click to a human user, but might obliterate several binary digits of a digital transmission. If the amplitude is kept constant, the frequency or phase of the carrier can be altered. This is more immune to noise since noise is more likely to affect the amplitude than the frequency or phase of the signal. If the frequency is being altered, then a binary zero might be represented by the transmission of a lower frequency carrier and a binary one by a higher frequency. Suppose the carrier has a nominal frequency of 1170 Hz, and we choose to deviate this by 100 Hz, then binary zero would be sent as a frequency of 1070 Hz whereas binary one would be sent as 1270 Hz. Since a digital message will always consist of binary ones or zeros the nominal carrier frequency of 1170 Hz will never actually be sent, (see Fig. 1.3).

If we keep both the amplitude and the frequency constant we can introduce changes of phase into the carrier signal. Since changes of phase are not so easy to detect as changes in amplitude or frequency, the phase change must be quite large. Fig. 1.3 shows a $180°$ phase change at each transition between the binary zero and binary one states. For all three types of modulation Fig. 1.3 only shows the effect of the modulation by the binary data signal on the carrier. With all

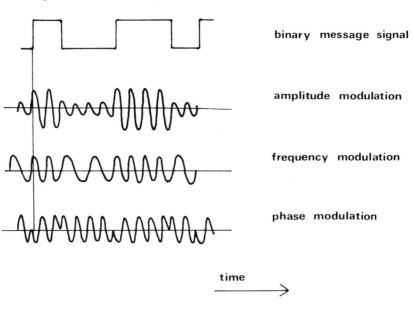

binary message signal

amplitude modulation

frequency modulation

phase modulation

time

Fig. 1.3.

these types of modulation other frequency components (called sidebands) are produced. The easiest type of modulation to explain the appearance of these other frequencies is amplitude modulation. If we consider a 1000 Hz carrier being amplitude modulated by a 10 Hz sinusoidal wave, the amplitude of the carrier wave will vary ten times per second. In this case the sidebands are produced by a simple process of addition and subtraction, giving rise to signals at 990 Hz on 1010 Hz. With both frequency and phase modulation the situation is more complex, and an infinite series of sidebands above and below carrier are produced at $\pm 2m$, $\pm 3m$, ... where m is the modulating frequency. The amplitude of these sidebands falls rapidly as their order increases. In order to be able to demodulate these signals to reproduce the original binary data correctly, the additional signals, termed sidebands, must be transmitted in addition to the carrier. It is this factor which limits the amount of data which can be sent through a channel.

We have so far described the effect on a sinusoidal carrier wave being modulated in various ways by a sinusoidal modulating signal. If the binary message consists of continuous one or zeros, then the carrier will have a constant amplitude frequency or phase with no sidebands being sent. If, at the other extreme, the binary message is constantly altering between binary one and zero, it is effectively a square wave with a frequency of half the bit rate in bits per second. With phase modulation, each transition of the binary message from one to zero or zero to one causes a phase change as before; with amplitude or frequency modulation the situation is more complex. Using a mathematical technique known as Fourier analysis, it can be shown that a square wave of frequency n can be decomposed to simple sinusoidal waves with a frequency of n, $3n$, $5n$ etc. whose amplitude decreases according to the function $\sin(x)/x$. This means that although theoretically a square wave has very many high frequency components their amplitude is very small. Transmitting components up to nine times the frequency of the modulating square wave should enable it to be accurately recovered. It can be seen then that modulation produces sidebands whose distribution depends on the frequency of the modulating signal, which itself will consist of a wide range of frequencies for a simple square wave. It is for this reason that rather sophisticated techniques must be used to send data at a reasonable rate. For example, low speed modems to connect terminals to computers normally use frequency modulation: two different carriers being sent on one channel to allow simultaneous communications in both directions. For higher speed links, typically for computer-to-computer links, phase modulation is used due to its lower bandwidth requirements. For speeds in excess of 2400 bits per second specially conditioned lines must be obtained from the communications authority. These are telephone lines whose bandwidth, distortion, and noise characteristics are within certain agreed limits. Some types of communications require modems which signal to both ends of a link the moment that the computer interface should either present or receive the next binary digit. In this case each modem must contain a clock which is kept in synchronism with the clock at the remote end of the line, by sending extra signals along the channel using further bandwidth. In some modems no separate clock signal is transmitted, the receiving modem synchonising its internal clock from the transitions in the received binary data. This system cannot work if continuous ones or zeros are sent, since there are no transitions in the received data to use for synchronisation. In this case the modems include a pseudo-random encoder and decoder to encode the data such that even if continuous ones or zeros are sent the signal still contains transitions.

CHAPTER 2

Transmission of Data

2.1 THE BYTE – AND WHAT IT MEANS

Most modern computers have as their smallest addressable memory unit the 8 bit byte. The term 'byte' does not in itself imply 8 bits, the 8 bit byte is simply the most common. These bytes may represent a binary number, or may be grouped together to store a large integer or real number; but for communications we normally use the value stored in each byte to represent a character. The values chosen to represent each character may be arbitrary provided they are used consistently. Since all communication with the outside world is by means of peripheral devices – such as line-printers, terminals, tape-readers etc. – it is important that these should all conform to the same standard – as must any software which needs to interpret data from them. For example, if the peripherals all interpret the characters A–Z as the values 20–45, but the software expected the range to be 10–35, the results would be confusing! This situation is not as rare as might be thought. Quite often the internal character set of a machine uses the full 8 bits of each byte – giving 256 possible characters, while many peripherals which might be connected to it accept only 7 bits as data and expect the 8th to be used as an error checking parity bit (see 2.5). One very popular range of machines uses its 36 bit words either as four 9 bit characters in inter-active mode, or as six 6 bit characters in batch mode!.

2.2 SOME CODES USED FOR DATA TRANSMISSION

2.2.1 The Baudot or Murray Code

The Murray code is an early code designed before 1925 for use with the then newly invented teleprinter. This is still the code used in today's telex service – the international dial-up telegraph network. The system was designed for use with slow mechanical teleprinters using only a 5 bit code; 5 bits allow only 32 possible combinations, so there are extended by means of a 'shift' system. In practice the code given by all zeroes is not used. The remaining 31 codes are used to represent the 26 letters of the alphabet, carriage-return, line-feed, space, figure-shift, and letter-shift. While the teleprinter is in letter-shift the codes representing A–Z cause the printing of the expected character; if a figure-shift character is received then the same codes cause the printing of an alternative character from the figure-shift set – 0–9, £, (,), etc., and continue to do so until another letter-shift is sent. With some teleprinters, return to letter-shift is automatic after a carriage-return, others do this after a space has been received. While the meaning of the codes used for the letter-shift is standard, there are more than ten variations in the assignment of the figure-shift codes, although the digits 0–9 are standard. The standard used in Britain and most of Europe is CCITT Alphabet #2. Much of the variation has occurred in the USA where, because of the lack of a state telecommunications monopoly, many communications companies devised their own variants —Western Union alone account for three of the variants (see Table. 2.1).

2.2.2 ASCII (American Standard Code for Information Interchange)

Although the 5 bit codes are widely used on the telex network for both intra- and inter-national communications, its limited character set and inefficient use of communications equipment and computer equipment, which is usually byte oriented, has led to the widespread acceptance of the ASCII code – defined by the American Standards Association (now known as the American National Standards Institute (ANSI)) in 1968.

The ASCII code is defined to use 7 bits, giving a possible 128 different codes. This number of codes allows the simple representation of all the upper and lower case letters, digits and a wide range of punctuation and special control characters (see Table 2.2).

Since the ASCII code uses only 7 out of the possible 8 bits, the 8th bit is often used as a parity bit for the detection of errors. It is normally set to 1 in systems not using parity.

The International Standards Organisation code ISO-7 is almost identical to ASCII; in everyday 'computer chat' the term ASCII is most commonly used but can quite often mean either.

2.2.3 EBCDIC (Extended Binary Coded Decimal Interchange Code)

This code occupies the full 8 bits in a byte and hence gives 256 possible characters. In practice, as can be seen from the table of EBCDIC codes, there are few extensions to the character set provided by ASCII, and many unused codes occur. Also inconvenient is the lack of continuity of the alphabetic codes which can make internal sorting of data stored in EBCDIC difficult. It is mainly used on IBM equipment but is also the internal code for data storage on the ICL 2900 machine range. EBCDIC is normally converted to ASCII before transmission through communications facilities since there are few peripherals which make use of EBCDIC. Table 2.3 shows the conversion from EBCDIC to ASCII recommended by the 'Blue book' (see 3.3.5). The use of all 8 bits of each byte makes

Table 2.1.

Octal value	Standard letter-shift	CCITT #2	USA AT and T	Western Union Telegraph
00				
01	E	3	3	3
02	LF	LF	LF	LF
03	A	—	—	—
04	SP	SP	SP	SP
05	S	'	Bell	Thru
06	I	8	8	8
07	U	7	7	7
10	CR	CR	CR	CR
11	D	Who are you	$	$
12	R	4	4	4
13	J	Bell	'	Bell
14	N	,		,
15	F		$\frac{1}{4}$	City
16	C	:	Who are you	:
17	K	(	$\frac{1}{2}$	(
20	T	5	5	5
21	Z	+	"	"
22	L	)	$\frac{3}{4}$	)
23	W	2	2	2
24	H		#	£
25	Y	6	6	6
26	P	0	0	0
27	Q	1	1	1
30	O	9	9	9
31	B	?	$\frac{5}{8}$	?
32	G		&	&
33	Figs	Figs	Figs	Figs
34	M	.	.	.
35	X	/	/	/
36	V	=	$\frac{3}{8}$	;
37	Ltrs	Ltrs	Ltrs	Ltrs

LF = line-feed; CR = carriage-return; SP = space; Figs = figure-shift; Ltrs = letter-shift.

Table 2.2 – ASCII Character Code.

Octal	Character	Octal	Character	Octal	Character	Octal	Character
0	NUL	40	Space	100	@	140	'
1	SOH	41	!	101	A	141	a
2	STX	42	"	102	B	142	b
3	ETX	43	#	103	C	143	c
4	EOT	44	$	104	D	144	d
5	ENQ	45	%	105	E	145	e
6	ACK	46	&	106	F	146	f
7	BEL	47	'	107	G	147	g
10	BS	50	(	110	H	150	h
11	HT	51	)	111	I	151	i
12	LF	52	*	112	J	152	j
13	VT	53	+	113	K	153	k
14	FF	54	,	114	L	154	l
15	CR	55	–	115	M	155	m
16	SO	56	.	116	N	156	n
17	SI	57	/	117	O	157	o
20	DLE	60	0	120	P	160	p
21	DC1	61	1	121	Q	161	q
22	DC2	62	2	122	R	162	r
23	DC3	63	3	123	S	143	s
24	DC4	64	4	124	T	164	t
25	NAK	65	5	125	U	165	u
26	SYN	66	6	126	V	166	v
27	ETB	67	7	127	W	167	w
30	CAN	70	8	130	X	170	x
31	EM	71	9	131	Y	171	y
32	SUB	72	:	132	Z	172	z
33	ESC	73	;	133	[	173	{
34	FS	74	<	134	\	174	|
35	GS	75	=	135	]	175	}
36	RS	76	>	136	∧	176	~
37	US	77	?	137	⊔	177	DEL

0-37 control characters; 141-172 can be interpreted as 101-132 on equipment without lower case facility; 177 is delete character.

parity checking of characters impossible. Table 2.4 shows the interpretation of the EBCDIC character code on the ICL 2900 machine range. Other manufacturers using EBCDIC have their own variations.

Table 2.3 – EBCDIC to ASCII Translation.

	0x	1x	2x	3x	4x	5x	6x	7x	8x	9x	Ax	Bx	Cx	Dx	Ex	Fx
x0	00	10			20	26	2D						7B	7D	5C	30
x1	01	11				2F	5E		61	6A			41	4A		31
x2	02	12	16						62	6B	73		42	4B	53	32
x3	03	13							63	6C	74		43	4C	54	33
x4									64	6D	75		44	4D	55	34
x5	09	NL	0A						65	6E	76		45	4E	56	35
x6		08	17						66	6F	77		46	4F	57	36
x7	7F		1B	04					67	70	78		47	50	58	37
x8		18							68	71	79		48	51	59	38
x9		19						60	69	72	7A		49	52	5A	39
xA					[¢]	21	[|]	3A								
xB	0B				2E	24	2C	23								
xC	0C	1C		14	3C	2A	25	40								
xD	0D	1D	05	15	28	29	5F	27					5B	5D		
xE	0E	1E	06		2B	3B	3E	3D								
xF	0F	1F	07	1A	7C	7E	3F	22								

The character NL has no direct equivalent; it must be replaced by the IA5 sequence CR followed by LF. The characters ¢ and | have no direct equivalents.

Table 2.4 – Showing Interpretation of the EBCDIC Character Code on the ICL 2900 Machine Range.

EBCDIC Hexa-decimal	Character	EBCDIC Hexa-decimal	Character
00	NULL	08	
01	Start Of Heading (TC1)	09	
02	Start of TeXt (TC2)	0A	
03	End of TeXt (TC3)	0B	Vertical Tabulate (FE3)
04		0C	Form Feed (FE4)
05	Horizontal Tabulate (FE1)	0D	Carriage Return (FE5)
06		0E	Shift Out
07	DELete	0F	Shift In

continued

Table 2.4 – *continued.*

EBCDIC Hexa-decimal	Character	EBCDIC Hexa-decimal	Character
10	Data Link Escape (TC7)	33	
11	Device Control 1	34	
12	Device Control 2	35	
13	Device Control 3	36	
14		37	End of Transmission (TC4)
15	New Line	38	
16	Back Space (FE0)	39	
17		3A	
18	CANcel	3B	
19	End of Medium	3C	Device Control 4
1A		3D	Negative ACKnowledge
1B			(TC8)
1C	IS4 (File Separator)	3E	
1D	IS3 (Group Separator)	3F	SUBstitute
1E	IS2 (Record Separator)	40	SPace
1F	IS1 (Unit Separator)	41	
20	Multiple SPace	42	
21	Multiple New Line	43	
22	Vertical Position	44	
23		45	
24		46	
25	Line Feed (FE2)	47	
26	End of Transmission Block (TC10)	48	
		49	
27	ESCape	4A	[(left bracket)
28		4B	. (fullstop)
29		4C	< (less than)
2A		4D	((left parenthesis)
2B		4E	+ (plus)
2C		4F	! (exclamation mark)
2D	ENQuiry (TC5)	50	& (ampersand)
2E	ACKnowledge (TC6)	51	
2F	BELL	52	
30		53	
31		54	
32	SYNchronous idle (TC9)	55	

continued

Table 2.4 – *continued.*

EBCDIC Hexa-decimal	Character	EBCDIC Hexa-decimal	Character
56		7A	: (colon)
57		7B	£ (pound)
58		7C	@ (at)
59		7D	' (apostrophe, acute)
5A	] (right bracket)	7E	= (equal)
5B	$ (dollar)	7F	" (double quote)
5C	* (asterisk)	80	
5D	) (right parenthesis)	81	a
5E	; (semicolon)	82	b
5F	∧ (circumflex)	83	c
60	– (minus)	84	d
61	/ (solidus)	85	e
62		86	f
63		87	g
64		88	h
65		89	i
66		8A	
67		8B	
68		8C	
69	| (vertical bar)	8D	
6A	¦ (broken vertical bar)	8E	
6B	, (comma)	8F	
6C	% (percentage)	90	
6D	_ (underline)	91	j
6E	> (greater than)	92	k
6F	? (question mark)	93	l
70		94	m
71		95	n
72		96	o
73		97	p
74		98	q
75		99	r
76		9A	
77		9B	
78		9C	
79	(grave)	9D	

continued

Table 2.4 – *continued.*

EBCDIC Hexa-decimal	Character	EBCDIC Hexa-decimal	Character
9E		C2	B
9F		C3	C
A0		C4	D
A1	~ (tilde)	C5	E
A2	s	C6	F
A3	t	C7	G
A4	u	C8	H
A5	v	C9	I
A6	w	CA	
A7	x	CB	
A8	y	CC	Prefix code
A9	z	CD	
AA		CE	
AB		CF	
AC		D0	} (right brace)
AD		D1	J
AE		D2	K
AF		D3	L
B0		D4	M
B1		D5	N
B2		D6	O
B3		D7	P
B4		D8	Q
B5		D9	R
B6		DA	
B7		DB	
B8		DC	
B9		DD	
BA		DE	
BB		DF	
BC		E0	\ (reverse solidus)
BD		E1	
BE		E2	S
BF		E3	T
C0	{ (left brace)	E4	U
C1	A	E5	V

continued

Table 2.4 – *continued.*

EBCDIC Hexa-decimal	Character		EBCDIC Hexa-decimal	Character	
E6	W		F3	3	
E7	X		F4	4	
E8	Y		F5	5	
E9	Z		F6	6	
EA			F7	7	
EB			F8	8	
EC			F9	9	
ED			FA		
EE			FB		
EF			FC		
F0	0 zero		FD		
F1	1		FE		
F2	2		FF		

2.4 CONTROL CHARACTERS

As has been seen, both ASCII and EBCDIC codes provide many special control characters. In the case of ASCII, all characters with values less than octal 40 are control characters; for EBCDIC the control characters are all allocated values less than hexadecimal 40. These control characters have special meanings in the context of serial synchronous transmission (see 2.7.4). They are used to frame messages to be sent between computer and computer, or computer and remote job entry terminal. This approach assumes that the user will never be allowed to send these special characters and will be restricted to those characters with a value greater than or equal to octal 40 in ASCII, or hexadecimal 40 in EBCDIC. In modern communications software, the user is allowed to send any character as data so other means of achieving 'transparency' – the ability to include any character in a message – have been developed (see 4.4.3).

The conventional meaning of some of the ASCII control codes is described in Table 2.5.

2.5 ERROR DETECTION

The simplest and most common means of detecting errors in data, when it has been either stored in the computer or transmitted over a data link, is the use of a parity bit. A parity bit is an extra bit of information added to the code for each character sent, in order to make the total number of binary 1's either always

Table 2.5 – Conventional Meaning of Some of the ASCII Control Codes.

Code	Meaning	Comments/Notes
NUL	Null	Used to fill in time for slow devices.
SOH	Start of Header	Indicates header information preceding data.
STX	Start of Text	The following characters form the text of a message.
ETX	End of Text	
EOT	End of Transmission	The link is being closed down.
ENQ	Enquiry	Requests the status of the system.
ACK	Acknowledge	The data was received correctly.
BEL	Bell	Rings an alarm bell.
BS	Back Space	Causes print position to move left one character.
HT	Horizontal Tabulate	Move print position to next horizontal tab. stop.
LF	Line Feed	Advance paper by one line.
VT	Vertical Tabulate	Advance paper to next vertical tab. stop.
FF	Form Feed	Advance paper to head of next form.
CR	Carriage Return	Move print position to column 'one'.
SO	Shift Out	Change to alternative 'shift' (character set).
SI	Shift In	Return to normal 'shift'.
DLE	Data Link Escape	Used to provide transparency.
DC1	Device Control 1	Used to perform device specific –
DC2	Device Control 2	Functions, for example, turn on and off the –
DC3	Device Control 3	Tape reader on a teleprinter.
DC4	Device Control 4	
NAK	Negative Acknowledge	The data was incorrectly received.
ETB	End of Text Block	Not yet a complete message.
CAN	Cancel	Ignore the last message.
EM	End of Media	Paper out in a line printer for example.
SUB	Substitute	
ESC	Escape	Used to gain the attention of a remote computer.
FS	File Separator	
GS	Group Separator	
RS	Record Separator	
US	Unit Separator	

odd, or always even, depending upon whether odd or even parity has been chosen. The mechanism is especially easy to implement where not all the 8 bits in a byte have been used, which is the case for ASCII, but not for EBCDIC. Some computers have hardware instructions for checking parity, or generating parity bits, which makes it very cheap in time and programming effort to use. Many peripherals such as teleprinters and VDUs check received parity and flag any characters received with invalid parity bit settings, and also send parity bits on data input by the keyboard for the remote computer to check: if the computer finds an error it will usually request that the character be re-entered. When ASCII data is transmitted with parity, the most significant bit is chosen as the parity bit — so that it may be easily removed to give the normal ASCII code value.

Table 2.6 shows the binary bit pattern for some ASCII characters with odd and even parity.

Table 2.6 — The binary bit pattern for some ASCII characters with odd and even parity.

Character	Even parity bit	Data 7 bits	Odd parity bit	Data 7 bits
A	0	1000001	1	1000001
B	0	1000010	1	1000010
C	1	1000011	0	1000011
1	1	0110001	0	0110001
2	1	0110010	0	0110010
3	0	0110011	1	0110011

A single parity bit can only check for the occurrence of a single erroneous bit in a character. If two erroneous bits are received, then a single parity bit will not show up the error. When data is sent in blocks of up to a few tens of characters, as it often is in data communications, the use of a block check character or longitudinal parity check is an added safeguard. This longitudinal parity bit is often called a 'checksum', and is arrived at in the same way as for 'vertical' parity described earlier.

Take for example the odd parity example showing the bit patterns for the ASCII characters ABC123 (see Table 2.7). Note that the parity bit on the block check character is calculated in the normal way, not by checking the parity of all the parity bits.

We shall discuss later practical efficient ways of implementing parity checking, the generation of block check characters of the longitudinal parity type, and also the use of cyclic redundancy checks which provide more efficient error detection (see 5.4.2.2).

Table 2.7.

Odd parity bit	Data 7 bits
A	1 1000001
B	1 1000010
C	0 1000011
1	0 0110001
2	0 0110010
3	1 0110011

Block check character	1 0001111

2.6 ERROR CORRECTION

The method used for the correction of errors found in data transmission varies according to the exact nature of the communication. In the case of a user typing on the keyboard of a terminal connected to a computer, if the computer finds a parity error in the data it receives, it can tell the user that a transmission error occurred, and request him to repeat the line. In the case of two computers communicating, then typically a block is transmitted to the sender after a block of data has been received, either to acknowledge correct receipt or to negatively acknowledge it, that is, to indicate an error has been detected. When a negative acknowledgement is received, the block of data which was incorrectly received is sent again. This scheme is called automatic repeat request, or ARQ and is used in some form in most inter-computer protocols. The use of ARQ implies that the medium upon which the transmission is taking place is capable of allowing transmission in either direction, though not necessarily simultaneously; this is called a 'duplex' channel. A channel which allows data to travel in both directions simultaneously is called 'full duplex'; if data can travel in either direction, but only one way at a time, it is called 'half duplex'. If the channel can only ever transmit in one direction it is called a 'simplex' channel, and obviously cannot use ARQ type error correction. An example of a simplex data transmission is that of Teletext, where data is sent 'piggy-back' on television broadcasts. Obviously a television receiver equipped with Teletext facilities cannot transmit a request for a repeat of data if an error occurs. In these cases the data may be repeated several times in the hope that if a character is received in error on its first transmission it will be correct on one of the subsequent transmissions. Alternatively the data can contain extra parity bits, allowing for detection of multiple bit errors, and correction of some of them. These codes are often so complex that as many parity bits as data bits are sent. This approach, in which redundant bits are sent to protect the information in the data bits, is called 'forward error correction'. Teletext uses a combination of 'forward error correction' – a 'Hamming code' and repetition, since all the pages transmitted are cycled through continuously taking 30 seconds or so between repetitions.

2.7 PARALLEL AND SERIAL TRANSMISSION

Having decided upon the character code that each end of a communication link will use, there are two possible ways of getting the data from the transmitter to the receiver; either in parallel, where each bit to be sent has a separate channel, or serially, where each bit is sent in turn down a single channel.

2.7.1 Parallel Transmission

With an 8 bit byte representing each character, we shall need 8 channels through which to send data, plus others to control the flow of data. Since parallel transmission uses so many channels it is only used for very local working, for local inter-computer links, or for connecting a computer to a local peripheral such as a line printer. Parallel transmission is restricted to small distances because it is costly to provide channels over long distances. To use parallel transmission on the public data network we would need to lease a telephone circuit for each channel we need, which would be very expensive.

A widely used parallel interface is the 'Centronics' printer interface, which is often used to connect local peripherals to microcomputer systems. Table 2.8 shows the designations and uses of the various lines provided on the Centronics interface.

2.7.2 Serial Transmission

Data consisting of characters which are each made up of several bits, must be sent along a single channel one bit at a time. This is often achieved by the use of a 'shift register'. A shift register is a device which can accept a complete byte of information in parallel, and then shift the data one bit at a time, detecting each bit as it 'falls off' the least significant end of the byte and sending it along the transmission channel (see Fig. 2.1).

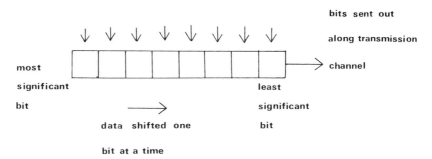

Fig. 2.1 – Operation of a shift register.

Table 2.8.

Line	Direction of signal		Function
	Transmitter	Receiver	
DB1 ⋮ DB8	⟶		8 bits of data, the 8th possibly representing parity.
DSTR	⟶		Data Strobe indicates that data is present to be read from the data lines.
ACK	⟵		Acknowledge indicates that the data has been received and more may be sent.
BUSY	⟵		Busy is sent in response to DSTR if the device is unable to receive this character, for example, due to buffer being full.
IBZ	⟵		Input Busy combines the signals on ACK and BUSY.
IP	⟶		Input Prime causes a reinitialisation of the receiver logic.
EMPTY	⟵		Indicates that the device buffer is completely empty.
ME	⟵		Media Error indicates out of paper conditions for a line printer, or tape in a tape punch.
SELECT	⟵		Indicates that this device is on-line, it is set off by either ME being set or the on-line switch being set off by an operator.
FAULT	⟵		A self detected fault has occurred in the receiver or device.

For reception, the same idea is used in reverse, bits being detected and shifted *in* one at a time from the communications channel moving toward the most significant end until a complete character has been received, when it can be read in parallel out of the register.

Since data when it is received is simply a stream of bits coming from the transmission channel, how do we know exactly where one character ends and the next begins? Two methods of achieving the necessary synchronization are used, called 'asynchronous' and 'synchronous' transmission. In the former characters are received with an unknown time interval between them and the last character received, whereas the latter describes a system where the arrival time of each character can be predicted.

2.7.3 Asynchronous Serial Transmission

Most mechanical peripherals such as teleprinters work in asynchronous mode. When data is sent by an asynchronous transmitter each character is preceded by a 'start' bit, and followed by 1, $1\frac{1}{2}$ or 2 'stop' bits.

The function of the start bit is to start a clock which will sample the line 8 times (to receive an 8 bit character) at a frequency determined by the speed of the transmission. The stop bit or bits are to allow the terminal to return to such a state that it can recognise a new start bit. A new start bit can occur immediately after the end of the stop bit, or after any period of time (see Fig. 2.2). If characters are sent as fast as possible in an asynchronous manner, there will be no time interval between the end of the stop bit and the beginning of the next start bit; such a speed is termed the 'cadence' speed of the transmitter.

Fig. 2.2 – Bits transmitted to send a character asynchronously.

The clock in the receiver must run at the determined signalling speed accurately enough to sample each data bit as near its centre as possible. Because the clock is only free running for 8 ticks before it is restarted it can be inaccurate by up to about 5% of the clock period without causing errors.

2.7.4 Synchronous Serial Transmission

In synchronous transmission a single clock is used to cause data to be shifted out of the shift register in the transmitter, and to control the time at which the line is sampled at the receiver so that the data may be shifted in. In the case of a transmitter and receiver which are quite close, the clock may be common to both and sent by a special line alongside the data, or if the data is sent by telephone lines then a modem which includes clock information in the transmission of the data must be used (see 1.3).

The provision of a common clock between the receiver and transmitter eliminates the need for start and stop bits on each character sent. When two stop bits and one start bit are added to each character on a line running at cadence speed, only 8/11ths of the capacity of the line is being used to send useful data. Synchronous transmission then, is much more efficient as it uses all the capacity usefully.

Since data bits are continuously being shifted into the receiver, some way needs to be found to indicate where the boundary of the first character actually lies. After the position of the first character has been found, subsequent ones can be obtained by shifting in multiples of 8 bits. The framing, or delimiting of the first character is achieved by use of a special synchronising (sync) character. This can be any character with an irregular bit pattern. In the ASCII character code it is named SYN and has octal value 26, that is, 00010110 in binary. EBCDIC also provides a sync character with value hexadecimal 32, that is, 00110010 in binary.

When the receiver is in the 'sync search' mode, that is, out of synchronization, it compares the value in its shift register with the bit pattern held in its 'sync register' to see if they are the same each time a bit is shifted in from the line. The software at the transmitter end arranges to send at least two SYN characters at the head of each message. The message could be several hundred characters long. The receiver software must switch the receiver into 'sync search' mode whenever it is expecting a message. When the bit patterns in the sync and receiver shift registers are the same, synchronization has been achieved, this causes a counter in the reciever to be started, which is incremented after each bit has been shifted in. When the clock has counted to 8, a 'receive done' status is set to indicate that a character has been assembled and should be removed for processing, the count is then reset.

In practice the receiver will contain another byte wide register into which the data byte is moved when all 8 bits have been read in. The software at the receiver can then read this register while the shift register is receiving the next 8 bits from the line. If this buffer register were not provided the receiver software would have only the time taken to receive one bit in which to remove the character from the interface when the 'receive done' flag is raised, whereas with a buffer register to allow double buffering it may take the time to receive a whole character to remove the data.

2.8 DATA TRANSMISSION SPEEDS: BITS PER SECOND AND BAUDS

The rate at which characters can be sent along a communications line is dependent on the number of binary information bits which can be sent in a given time; the number of bits used to represent each character; and the number of bits which need to be sent in addition to the data.

The basic capacity for information transfer on a line is measured in bits per second; the term 'baud' is often used synonymously, but it has a slightly different meaning. The term baud used correctly describes the rate at which the signal on the communications line alters its state. For the case where the line signal is in one of two states to represent a single binary digit the terms baud and bits per second are equivalent.

If we consider a case where a modem sends one of four different signal levels, so that the four levels represent 2 bits each, that is, 00, 01, 10, 11, then each signal element will represent 2 bits, and so the signalling baud rate will be half the information transfer rate in bits per second.

Since most data communications equipment is designed to use 8 bit codes we shall consider the character rate for this case. For an asynchronous line working at a data transmission rate of 1200 bits per second, sending 8 bit bytes, plus 1 start bit and 2 stop bits per character, that is, 11 bits per character in total the peak character rate is 1200/11 per second (about 110 cps). For the synchronous case the rate is 1200/8 per second (or 150 cps).

2.9 CONNECTING TOGETHER COMPUTER COMMUNICATIONS EQUIPMENT

Communications equipment that is sited at any distance greater than a few hundred feet from the equipment with which it is communicating will be connected either by a telephone line with a modem at each end, or if the range is only a few hundred feet by a 'modem eliminator', also known as a base band modem or long-line driver. If the distance to be covered is very small then all that is required is a null modem in order to simulate to both ends of the link the signals that would be provided in addition to the data by a modem. It will be described after the control signals provided by a modem have been explained. As we saw in Chapter 1, the function of the modem is to convert the serial stream of data bits into signals that can be sent on ordinary voice grade telephone lines. The modem eliminator is used where the user of a communications link is able to install his own short link between two sites and the data stream does not need to be converted to audio signals, but can be sent as it stands, with some amplification and shaping to improve matters.

2.9.1 V.24/RS232-C

Almost all data communications equipment is built to operate using certain standard definitions of what signals should be provided, at what level, and by whom. The two bodies that issue these specifications are the CCITT in Europe, and EIA in the USA. The most widely used specifications are the CCITT recommendation V.24 or the EIA RS232-C. These specifications contain the electrical signal characteristics, mechanical interface details, descriptions of the function of each signal, and lists of standard subsets for use in varying applications. Table 2.9 shows the most widely used subsets of V.24/ RS232-C signals.

The minimum usable subset of the V.24 signals is indicated by the absence of a letter in the subset column of the V.24/RS232-C function table. This subset would permit communication to be established over a private permanent circuit using asynchronous transmission. To use the dial-up telephone system one should add the two signals indicated by "D" in the subset column. To use synchronous transmission the control of signals marked by "S" is required, except that only one of each of the pairs linked by braces are required. The abbreviations DTE and DCE are widely used in communications parlance to indicate Data Terminal Equipment (that is, a computer or terminal) and Data Communication Equipment, the modem or line interface. Note that one often finds equipment described as 'V.24 or RS232-C compatible' even though it provides less than the minimum subset, this can cause problems.

Table 2.9 — The Most Widely Used Subsets of V.24/RS232-C Signals.

Reference designation		Function name	Subset
RS232-C	V.24		
AA	101	Protective Ground	
AB	102	Reference Ground	
BA	103	Transmitted Data	
BB	104	Received Data	
CA	105	Request to Send	
CB	106	Clear to Send	
CC	107	Data Set Ready	
CD	108/2	Data Terminal Ready	D
CE	125	Ring Indicator	D
CF	109	Carrier Detect	
CG	110	Signal Quality Detector	S
CH	111	Data Signal Rate Select — DTE Source	S⎞
CI	112	Data Signal Rate Select — DCE Source	S⎠
DA	113	Transmitter Timing — DTE Source	S⎞
DB	114	Transmitter Timing — DCE Source	S⎠
DD	115	Receiver Timing	S

D = Dial-up switched network; S = Synchronous communications.

2.9.2 What the Signal Names Mean

Protective Ground and *Reference Ground* are used to connect terminal equipment to the modem, the former for electrical safety, the latter to provide a reference level against which the state of the other lines can be judged to be either on or off.

Transmitted Data (TxD) provides the lines upon which the data terminal presents data to the modem, the *Received Data* (RxD) line presents data received by the modem to the data terminal.

Request To Send (RTS) must be set whenever the data teminal wishes to transmit data — it may not do so until the modem sets *Clear To Send* (CTS). In full duplex applications it is normal to keep Request To Send permanently set, even if data is only to be sent periodically. In the case of half duplex circuits the time delay between the terminal asserting Request To Send and the modem returning Clear To Send is used to ensure that the distant modem is in a state suitable for receiving data, it is set in the modem to be between about 20 milliseconds and 250 milliseconds. In order for a modem in half duplex working to receive data, its Request To Send line must first be dropped. The time taken to alter from receive to transmit mode in half duplex is called the turn-round time. To avoid these delays it is best to run the communications equipment in full duplex mode if possible, even if the data to be transmitted is half duplex in nature, that is, always alternating between sending and receiving data.

Data Set Ready (*DSR*) is used to indicate that the modem is switched on and in normal functioning mode, not in a test state etc.

Carrier Detect (*CD*) indicates that the modem is receiving a signal from the telephone line which appears to be emanating from another compatible modem. It should stay set whenever data is being received; if a gap of more than a few milliseconds occurs it will be unset indicating that connection has been lost. If carrier disappears for a transient period due to noise on the telephone line this is not signalled and it is up to the error detection in the software to note that errors have occurred. These small transients may however cause the *Signal Quality Detector* (*SQ*) line to be unset, indicating a high probability that data errors will be found.

Data Terminal Ready (*DTR*) is set by the terminal to signify that it is ready to operate. It is used on dial-up connections to answer and maintain the call — equivalent to keeping the handset off the hook on an ordinary telephone call. Unsetting Data Terminal Ready causes a call to be terminated — equivalent to hanging up on a telephone call.

Ring Indicator (*RI*) is used when a modem is connected to the dial-up telephone network and is equipped to answer incoming calls. When a ringing tone is detected on the line, which would normally cause a bell to ring in a telephone, this line is raised. Ring Indicator is unset at all times except when the ringing tone is present, it is off between rings. In order to answer an incoming call, the terminal or computer should raise Data Terminal Ready and check that Carrier Detect is set on a small time after Data Terminal Ready was set on; a digital 'conversation' may then ensue, followed by unsetting Data Terminal Ready to terminate the connection.

Synchronous communications, as we have seen, requires a clock signal to be supplied to the transmitter and receiver simultaneously to cause the data bits to be sent out and detected at the correct times. This clock may be provided in either modem, or in the terminal interface. In practice most modems provide the clock, but if the synchronous communications connection is a very local one then it may not be worth the expense of a modem; a clock is still needed however, and can often be supplied as an optional extra on the communications interface on the terminal or computer so that a null modem may still be used (see 2.9.3). If the clock signals are supplied by the modem, the clock is said to be in the DCE source, or if in the terminal or computer, the DTE source.

If the clock is within the modem, the timing signals necessary to control the terminals communications interface are set on the *Transmitter Signal Element Timing (DCE Source)* line, whereas, if the clock is in the terminal, it is sent to the modem on the *Transmitter Signal Element Timing (DTE Source)* line. Only one of these two signals may be present.

Very often the clock in the modem or terminal is switchable between two speeds, normally the higher is used but when many data errors are encountered due to noise it may be switched to the lower speed for more robust communication. This signal is sent from the modem or terminal to indicate to the other which speed has been chosen using either *Data Signalling Rate Select (DCE Source)* *(DSRS – DCE)* or *Data Signalling Rate Select (DTE Source) (DSRS – DTE)*. The set state of the line indicates the higher of the two speeds. Typical speeds might be 1200 and 2400 baud on a dial-up line, or 4800 and 9600 baud on a leased line.

Irrespective of whether the modem or the terminal supplies the clock signal at the transmitter end of the synchronous communications link, it is recovered from the signal received at the receiver end modem and presented to the receiving communications interface on the *Receiver Signal Element Timing* line to control the shifting in of data from the modem.

2.9.3 The Null Modem

In order for two closely located pieces of data communications equipment to communicate, both ends must be fooled into believing they are connected to a modem. This is simplest for the Asynchronous case where no clocks are involved. Pin numbers for the standard "D" connectors used with V.24/RS232-C communications equipment (see Fig. 2.3).

The reasons for the particular interconnections and crossovers should be apparent if the reader has fully grasped the meanings of the signals on the V.24 interface.

In order to operate a synchronous data link without a modem clock signals need to be supplied. The Receiver Signal Element Timings is accepted on pin 17,

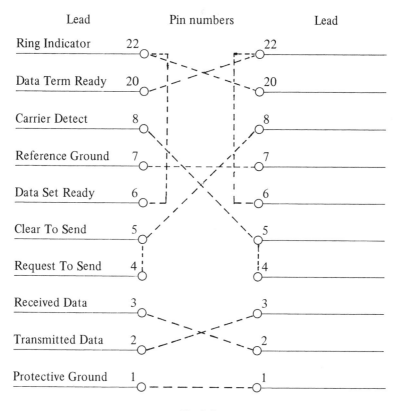

Lead	Pin numbers		Lead
Ring Indicator	22	22	
Data Term Ready	20	20	
Carrier Detect	8	8	
Reference Ground	7	7	
Data Set Ready	6	6	
Clear To Send	5	5	
Request To Send	4	4	
Received Data	3	3	
Transmitted Data	2	2	
Protective Ground	1	1	

Fig. 2.3.

this should be connected to pin 15 on the other device, where Transmitter Signal Element Timing (DTE Source) is provided, and the converse arrangement for the other direction, that is:

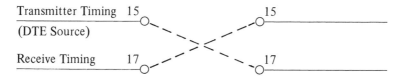

Transmitter Timing (DTE Source)	15	15
Receive Timing	17	17

The connection on the other leads is as before. Both ends of the data link must be equipped with the clock option present in the synchronous communications interface.

If neither device contains a clock the timing signals must be provided from elsewhere. A 'modem eliminator' may be used; this fulfils the function of a null modem with the addition of providing clock signals to both ends of the data link.

2.9.4 Dial-Up Versus Leased Lines

The use of the dial-up network as against private leased lines is dependent on two factors: the usage, and the facilites required.

The usage determines whether it is financially advantageous to pay telephone charges at the normal rate or to lease a line for a fixed annual rental. Some typical leased line rental charges are given for Tariff "T" circuits provided by British Telecom as at February 1981.

Length km	Connection charge	Annual rental
1	£120	£231
10	£120	£888
100	£160	£1820
>480	£180	£4500

To install a long leased line may take at least 3–6 months from ordering to delivery. A leased line may be used with a privately owned modem and will be terminated with a four wire connection, allowing full duplex operation. A dial-up line only terminates with a two wire connection, hence only half duplex operating is possible.

A typical modem for leased line synchronous operation is the Racal 48/96, which will operate either at 9600 bits per second full duplex, or with the addition of an optional card, as two full duplex 4800 bits per second channels simultaneously. For dial-up lines most PTTs (Post, Telephone and Telegraph authorities) can supply modems for synchronous operation at 600, 1200, or 2400 bits per second in half duplex mode only. For asynchronous working modems which operate at 300 and 1200 bits per second, full duplex are available for communicating with terminals similarly equipped or equipped with acoustic couplers. Both types can be equipped to automatically answer incoming calls.

The acoustic coupler is a device which enables data to be sent using an ordinary telephone. This is done cradling the handset of the telephone in a special holder which enables the modem to 'talk' and 'listen', without being electrically connected.

CHAPTER 3

Physical Network Techniques

3.1 NETWORK TOPOLOGIES

The shape or topology of computer networks is dictated both by the geographical locations of the centres to be connected, and the logical structure of the organisation creating the network. The types of protocol being employed may influence the design; use of the latest CCITT standard protocols should remove this constraint, as they are more general than older, manufacturer-specific protocols.

The exact nature of each link in a network depends on the physical requirements, and what is permissible or available for use at each location. Typically, networks consist of telephone circuits rented from a telecommunications company. If the connections to be made are short it may be possible to install the lines personally. In the case of a particularly remote site it may be necessary to install a radio or microwave link.

No matter what physical medium is used to make a communication link it will ultimately convert received signals to standard levels on a known interface, such as V.24 (see 2.9.1).

3.1.1 Point to Point Links

The simplest type of computer communications is that in which only two systems or locations are involved. There are no choices to be made about the route of the link, as only a single two-way direct connection is required. The connection might be between two different types of computer located either close together, or far apart. The link may be required to transport files of information or to pass messages from one real time system to another. The two computers may have different character sets, or use different character codes; there are often many such trivial problems to overcome. Alternatively, it may be that the submission of jobs, for example, on cards, and the reception of results by a line printer — some distance from the central computer (remote job entry) is required. In this case, provision must be made for communicating with the operators on the central computer, or alternatively, directly with the operating system so that enquiries about, and modification to jobs submitted, can be made.

If interactive access is required to the central computer, then several terminals may share one line for economic reasons, in which case the sharing of the line may be implemented either by a small computer called a concentrator, or terminal control processor, or by a variety of types of multiplexor which perform a similar task using hardware.

3.1.2 Multidropped Lines

In situations where several terminals or remote job entry stations require access to a central computer, and lie on a direct path from the most remote site to the central facility, it may be possible to install a single line with several connections to it along its length.

In Fig. 3.1 such a route is shown: a single leased line from Manchester to London passes through the centres shown, locations on the route being connected to the same line, thus avoiding the expensive duplication otherwise involved in linking these four remote locations. In order to use this multidrop configuration of circuit, the equipment at each site must be capable of recognising when the central computer or master is addressing it in order to send it data, or requesting

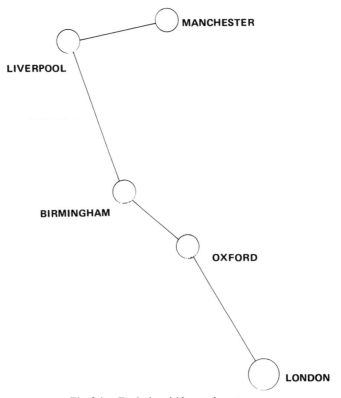

Fig. 3.1 – Typical multidropped route.

that data should be sent back. The 7020 protocol has the capacity to use multi-dropped lines for remote job entry. This is described in Chapter 5, where the detail of the mechanism used can be found. If interactive terminal access is required at each location, then special terminals are required which can buffer an entire message while it is being input. They must also recognise the appropriately addressed message from the master instructing it to send the message in its buffer, or display the data contained in an incoming message for the user. These terminals are quite costly compared with simple 'glass teletype' VDUs. If several terminals are required at one site it is generally cheaper to use simple VDUs in association with a concentrator of some kind rather than the intelligent terminals otherwise required.

3.2 MESSAGE SWITCHING

So far, the network topologies we have considered have been limited by having a direct link from the remote to the central locations. Although a multidropped line may pass through many locations, it still fulfils this characteristic as only one location makes use of the whole line at any time. For a heavily centralised organisation it may be satisfactory to communicate with all its distant branches by point to point, or multidroppped lines. If the branches of an organisation need to communicate with one another it is inefficient to go via the central branch when the branches may actually be quite close together. The inefficiencies created by the imposition of a centralised network on a homogenous organisation were first recognised by the telephone companies. It is obviously absurd to connect all subscribers in Britain to a single giant exchange in London when the majority of calls are local. The telephone companies have evolved a mesh network: it is not simply hierarchical, with subscribers connected to local exchanges; local exchanges connected to area exchanges; areas to trunks and so on, but also contains cross connections at all levels for heavily used routes – see Fig. 3.2.

From the late 1920s onwards teleprinter links become more popular, to such an extent that there is a public teleprinter network which parallels the telephone network – the Telex system. Some large organisations also evolved their own private teleprinter networks, in which each branch is only connected to a few of its nearest sister branches. When a message is to be sent from one branch to another, the destination is added to the head of the message, then it is sent to the next branch connected in the direction of its destination. When the message is received at this intermediate branch it is both typed out, and punched onto paper tape. The operator then takes this paper tape, and, having read the destination address from the typed copy, sends it either to the next branch en route, or to the final destination if it is directly connected. Thus for a message to be sent a long distance, it might be transcribed onto paper tape and then sent on many times. This 'torn tape' switching system illustrates a crude message switching system which was emulated by early computer networks of the store

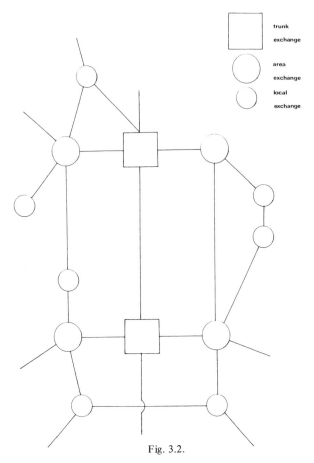

Fig. 3.2.

and forward type. It simply replaced the operator reading the destination address by placing it in a fixed place in the message in a known format, so that the computer could forward the complete message to the next branch, or 'network node'.

The manual 'torn tape' system uses a skilled operator to perform several tasks which must be handled by software in a computerised network node. The most important of these tasks are routing and network information distribution. In the manual system the operator will probably have a routing table in his memory, possibly referring to a diagram for less common destinations. Sometimes some parts of the network are more heavily used than others and queues of tapes to be sent down a particular channel may occur. Probably there will be several routes to each destination, some longer in distance than others, or going through more switching centres, so the operator at each centre must use his knowledge to route messages in the optimum way. Often there is insufficient information at a node to know which route is optimal; it may be that the next node on the direct route is overloaded, making it more efficient to use an alternative route even though the channel connecting to the next node is not in itself overloaded. To be able to make sensible decisions about dynamic routing we need a mechanism for network information distribution. This (information distribution) may either be in the form of special messages sent by the same mechanisms through the network, or it may use a different parellel network. If the network itself is used to distribute network information, there needs to be a mechanism for ensuring that this takes priority over ordinary 'user' messages, possibly having the power to abort the transmission of a user message if the information is imperative. In the torn tape switching centre, the prioritising or pre-empting is performed by the operator; alternatively the telephone system may be used as the network for the transmission of network information. Ideally, network information concerning overloading or breakdown should be sent to every node in a network to aid the optimisation of dynamic routing algorithms, informing only directly connected nodes may provide a workable but suboptimal solution.

3.3 PACKET SWITCHING

In message switching systems communications channels can be quite efficiently utilised; the overhead resulting from the appending of the destination address to the message is usually small compared to the total size of the message. When loading in these types of systems exceeds about 80% of their maximum capacity they become very slow. If a long message of several thousand characters is sent through a fairly slow speed channel it will block other messages for a considerable time. When many long messages are being simultaneously sent, the network can become unstable, that is, the transit time through the network does not increase linearly with increased load; above a certain threshold it increases very rapidly.

Packet switching is designed to both remove the instability of transit time with increasing load, and prevent the delays caused by sending long messages over limited capacity communications channels. This is achieved by splitting messages up into small fixed size pieces (called packets), each with the destination address contained therein. In networks using dynamic routing, the packets are also given a sequence number so that they can be reassembled into coherent messages, even if the constituent packets making up a message have been sent by different routes and have taken different times to reach their destination.

Networks employing packet switching usually have a mesh type of topology in which all the nodes are indirectly connected with each other via links between some adjacent nodes. The decisions about which nodes to connect, and what capacity of channels to employ is very complex; the reader is referred to a more theoretical work. Packet switched systems have been in use for some time and it seems likely that they will dominate computer communications in the future. The public telephone systems were once entirely analogue, using only amplifiers or repeaters for long distance routes to maintain signal levels. The problems with analogue connections between distant locations are distortion and noise. Random noise is a characteristic of all electronic circuits except when at a temperature of absolute zero; impulsive noise also results from faulty switching, or can be induced by switching adjacent lines. When repeated amplification is applied to already noisy signals, it both amplifies existing noise and introduces further noise. There is thus a limit to the number of times a signal can be repeatedly amplified before the signal is lost in noise. This is not the case in digital circuits: a device called a regenerative repeater is used at points along a channel where the signal is becoming attenuated or noisy. This device has only to sense whether or not a pulse is present at a particular instant; if it decides a pulse is present, it then creates a new accurately-shaped pulse at its output. Thus digital links can be made over long distances with no distortion or added noise. Telephone companies had been using digital transmission long before computer networks created a requirement, by digitising speech on long distance trunk networks where noise and distortion are most critical. Digitising is performed by sampling the speech waveform at a rate greater than twice the maximum frequency to be sent, typically 8000 times per second on a telephone speech circuit responding from 300–3500 Hz. At each of the 8000 instants per second, the wave form is sampled and a value between 0 and 127 is assigned, depending on the logarithm of its amplitude. This number can be represented by seven binary bits, with an eighth bit added to carry control information. Thus a voice channel carried digitally requires a channel capacity of $8 \times 8000 = 64$ K bps. Many of these channels can be sent over a single cable, waveguide or optical fibre using a technique called multiplexing which is described later (see 3.5). Presently, a long distance data link will start as a digital signal in the computer; it will then be converted to an analogue signal by a modem; travel to an exchange and be reconverted to a digital form. The inverse process applies at the other end. The fastest data signalling rate used on ordinary voice grade channels is about 9.6 K bps due to limitations in the conversion of digital signals to analogue, and vice versa. Thus, although trunk channels send data of 64 K bps, we can presently only use up to 9.6 K bps, unless we lease multiple channels thus multiplying the capacity available to us. This wasteful situation is being remedied as new electronic exchanges are brought in for use, even at local exchange level in the UK with the introduction of 'System X', or 'Data Phone Digital Service' (DDS) of the US Bell company. With these systems it is possible to bring the digital network to the subscriber without any need for modems or an analogue subscriber to exchange line. This widespread access to a public digital telephone network has initiated the development by the CCITT of a series of important specifications for a public packet switched network, best known of which is the X.25 interface standard. This worldwide standard is now in use in PSS in the UK, Transpac in France and Datapac in Canada. X.25 is sufficiently strong and widespread that all manufacturers of computer equipment with any pretensions to communicate will be compelled to adopt it.

3.3.1 X.25 The International Packet Switching Standard

Recommendation X.25 of the CCITT provides a worldwide standard interface for packet switched networks, public or private. It provides three specifications for physical, link, and packet level interfaces. The physical interface to digital networks is fully defined in definition X.21. Until the use of digital connection direct to subscribers becomes widespread, X.21 bis which is compatible with V.24 is to be used. The link level defines the protocol to be used to provide error free transparent transmission of packets. It uses cyclic redundancy checks and sequence counts to protect the data, and operates in full duplex mode. This protocol predates X.25 and is called HDLC (High Level Data Link Control). The physical and link level protocols could be replaced with some other procedures to provide a transparent communications interface. It is the packet level which characterises the network users view of X.25.

The packet level specification of X.25 allows the user to send datagrams or to communicate over permanent virtual circuits (PVCs) or by virtual calls (VCs). These are analogous with telegrams, leased lines and dial-up connections in the public telephone system. The packet level interface divides up a single physical channel into 15 groups of 255 logical channels each. The group number is identified by 4 bits and the channel number by 8 bits in the header on each packet. The software used to implement levels 2 and 3, the link and packet levels of X.25 will normally be within the computer connected to the network. The software will direct the data or control information from packets with a given channel number to the appropriate process in the computer.

Fig. 3.3 illustrates a connection between process A and process B in different computers attached to the network. The association between group 1 channel 131 in computer 1 and group 2 channel 243 in computer 2 may either represent a PVC, set up by arrangement with the operators of the network, or a VC, set up when communications between processes A and B are required. Setting up a virtual call is achieved by exchanging special call set-up packets between the two computers, and call termination by other control packets. The computer which wishes to set up a virtual call chooses the highest numbered free logical channel, and sends a packet containing explicitly the address of the remote system it wishes to connect with. The remote computer receives incoming connections on the lowest numbered free logical channel. If it is able to receive this incoming connection it will send a call accepted packet. From then on data packets sent into these logical channels at either end of the connection will automatically be routed to the other without specific mention of the destination address.

3.3.2 High Level Protocols

The packet or network level interface just described allows two systems on a network to communicate with each other; it does not provide a very high level interface. It is up to the user to block his data into packets of the correct size

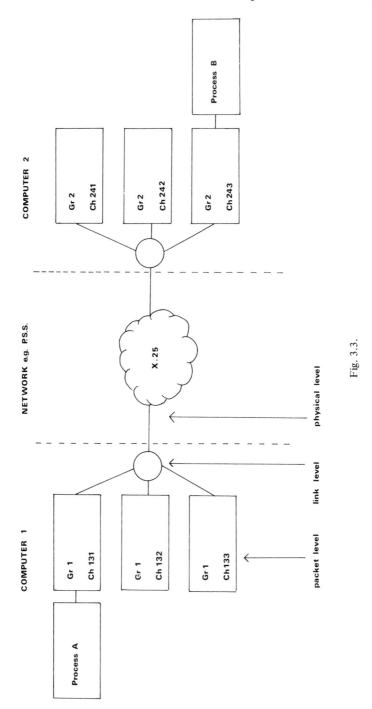

Fig. 3.3.

and set up and maintain calls. The addressing used in X.25 to connect to a remote system also assumes that the remote process being accessed is on the same network, and not connected on another interconnected network, in which case further addressing information will be needed. It is unlikely that communications technology will stop with X.25 systems; there are always newer, better systems on the horizon, requiring an interface which will remain constant even if the underlying communications technology alters. These functions are provided by a Transport Service which defines a set of procedures called from within a program on a computer to address and communicate with other systems, possibly on the other interconnected networks. Such a definition has been produced by British Telecom PSS Study Group 3, which will probably form the basis for an international standard. This definition is often referred to as 'Yellow Book Transport Service'.

Certain operations making use of a network between two systems are so frequent that standards have been defined for their implementation, particularly interactive terminal access to remote systems, file transfer, and remote job entry. The CCITT has three recommendations relating to terminal access across packet switched networks; X.3, X.28 and X.29 (known collectively as Triple X). British Telecom study groups have provided definitions for file transfer and job submission.

3.3.3 Transport Service Facilities

The Transport Service (TS) interface will be the level at which most future communications programmers will access networks. The ways in which programming languages allow access to the facilities will be varied; perhaps initially through a procedure call, but later probably incorporating the facilities into new languages. The facilities provided by TS could be supplied by any packet switched network system, apart from those based on X.25, hence we have both forward compatibility with new systems, and retrospective compatibility, whereby existing networks can provide compatible functions by the addition of TS software.

The most important facilities provided in TS are named:

CONNECT	DISCONNECT
ACCEPT	RESET
DATA	EXPEDITED
PUSH	

CONNECT is used by a process attempting to establish communications with another process. An address field specifies the logical route to be used, possibly crossing from one network to another and ultimately to the remote process required. If the remote process decides to accept the incoming CONNECT request it returns ACCEPT; to reject the request it returns DISCONNECT. DISCONNECT is also used to terminate a connection between two processes.

The DATA function may be used by either end of a link to send data through the network to the other process after a CONNECT has been accepted. PUSH ensures that all data sent by a process is received. It is used whenever a response from the remote process is required, by causing any data held in intermediate buffers to be forced out. RESET may be generated by either end of a link or by the network. The effect of RESET is to abandon any waiting messages on a link, its use is to indicate catastrophic failure requiring a process to restart at a known point or in a known state. If it is generated by the network it will be to report a breakdown or data loss by an intermediate node in the network link. A pair of RESETs will be sent, one to each end of the link, to indicate to both ends the failure that has occurred. The EXPEDITED facility is used to rush a message at high priority to the remote process, possibly overtaking any other messages in transit. It is used to provide an interrupt facility where a message must be sent in response to some event occurring in real time.

These TS facilities will provide a constant interface for the writers of applications programs with a need to communicate, and will also protect other high level protocols which use TS from changes in the mechanisms used to provide the network function.

3.3.4 Character Terminal Protocols

The CCITT 'Triple X' (X.3/X.28/X.29) proposals specify how simple terminals such as VDUs and teletypes may access computers on an X.25 network. Simple terminals send one character at a time as soon as a key has been depressed, using asynchronous transmission. To enable such a terminal to communicate via a packet switched network, it is connected to a small computer whose function is to assemble completed messages into packets and to receive packets and disassemble them in order to send the data contained to the terminal. This function is called Packet Assembly-Disassembly and is performed by a device known as a PAD. The PAD is also responsible for prompting a user to give the network address required, performing echoing and local editing such as delete character or line, and providing padding characters to slow mechanical terminals to allow sufficient time for carriage return or horizontal tabulate without losing subsequent characters. CCITT recommendation X.3 specifies the various parameters which may be set in a PAD to best serve a particular terminal type; X.28 details the terminal/PAD interface, recommending special control characters for example, and X.29 specifies the way in which a PAD and host computer system communicate using X.25 packets.

It should be noted that the CCITT recommendations map the control and encoding of messages to be sent to hosts directly into X.25 packets, with no mention of a transport service. This causes two serious problems: it can only be used in X.25 based networks; and the limited addressing scope of X.25 means that communications via gateways to host computers on other networks is not easily possible. The British Telecom PSS Study Group 3 have produced a specification of how the Triple X proposals will be used in British Telecom's PSS, and also a mapping of X.29 onto the network independent Transport Service termed TS.29. The use of two protocols obviously requires the use of protocol conversion to allow connections to be made with only one or other of the protocols implemented. X.29 will be widely implemented initially, it is expected therefore that sites using TS.29 will also have X.29 facilities or a protocol converter.

In order to control complex terminals with one or several pages of text stored in them, and internal facilities to manipulate the text, a virtual terminal protocol will be required. To date, however, no widely recognised protocol for this function exists.

3.3.5 Job Submission and File Transfer Protocols

Apart from remote terminal access, file transfer is probably the most widely used function of a network. Job submission can be considered as a special case of file transfer in which job control records, possibly together with programs or data, are sent to a remote computer, not to be stored permanently in filestore, but to be executed as commands. Any output produced by a job can also be treated as a file whose destination may be the filestore of the computer from which the job was submitted, or a lineprinter or graph plotter. It is not even necessary that the computers involved have secondary storage devices onto which the file may be spooled for subsequent printing, but may simply be remote job entry computers equipped only with slow peripherals such as card readers and lineprinters. No international file transfer protocol specification is expected until the mid 1980s, but the Data Communications Protocols Unit of the National Physical Laboratory in England have produced a comprehensive specification called FTP-80. This protocol is based on experience gained with an earlier version used on SRC-net. This specification is expected to form the basis of the future international standard. FTP-80 describes the filestore of each machine on which it is implemented in terms of a virtual filestore defined by a set of attributes detailing both the way the file is stored and how it is to be transferred. FTP-80 uses the network independent TS described earlier to perform the data transmission required, and is thus not limited in use to single X.25 networks. Unlike the character terminal protocol, FTP-80 does not detail the user interface, recognising that according to circumstances it may run as a single user program; as a task responding to a queue of user requests; or as a component of an operating system with an interface to the job control language of the computer. FTP-80 specifies many options to permit a wide range of efficient transfer mechanisms; it also specifies a minimum subset so that all implementations should be able to transfer simple text files.

Apart from file transfer, file access and file manipulation have also been recognised as areas where high level protocols could usefully exist. A file access protocol would specify mechanisms by which a process in a computer remote from the site of the data it needs to operate on can read, write or delete specific records of a file. File manipulation protocols would permit remote listing of filestore directories, deletion and renaming of files located in a remote computer system. As there have not yet emerged any clear contenders which might form the basis for future international standardisation, no examples have been cited.

3.4 TERMINAL CONTROL PROCESSORS AND CONCENTRATORS

In any computer system where the users are clustered into groups geographically remote from a central computer facility, it makes economic sense to connect each of the cluster of users by a local line to a small communications computer which will assemble messages from each and send them down a single high speed line to the central computer. To connect n 300 bps terminals using a single high speed line we do not need a line capacity of $n \times 300$ bps but very much less. This is because most terminals are inactive for most of the time and it would be a rare event for all terminals on such a terminal control processor (TCP) to be active simultaneously. The speed of line chosen to connect to the central computer will be also determined to an extent by the delays in response which a user will tolerate if his message has to queue for a significant time in the TCP. The TCP will be responsible for character echoing and local editing such as character or line deletion; in the case of an X.25 connection the term packet assembler-disassembler (PAD) is used to describe a TCP (see 3.3.4). Financial savings may be gained by using one high speed line rather than many slow speed lines for each group of users, which for a large time-sharing bureau could be very large. Computer systems also use TCPs to relieve the central computer of the burden of dealing with every single character as a key is depressed; instead it passes complete messages terminated by some agreed delimiter, for example, carriage return. In some cases, all of a computer systems input/output is handled by a communications computer called a front-end processor (FEP) which may be connected directly to the main memory of the computer system. In this way the FEP will only be required to wake-up or interrupt the main computer once to inform it that a complete message has been received or sent (see Fig. 3.4).

Where several devices other than terminals (for example, line printers) or other TCPs are being connected by a single high speed line to a central computer, the more general term 'concentrator' is used. A concentrator's function is essentially one of collecting data from several services and interleaving it down a single communications channel in such a way that the central computer can disentangle the separate conversations. This is typically effected by assigning an address to each data source or sink (destination) and prefixing each message with this address.

3.5 MULTIPLEXORS

Multiplexing is the division of a transmission channel into several sub-channels. This function is performed by software in concentrators and by hardware or

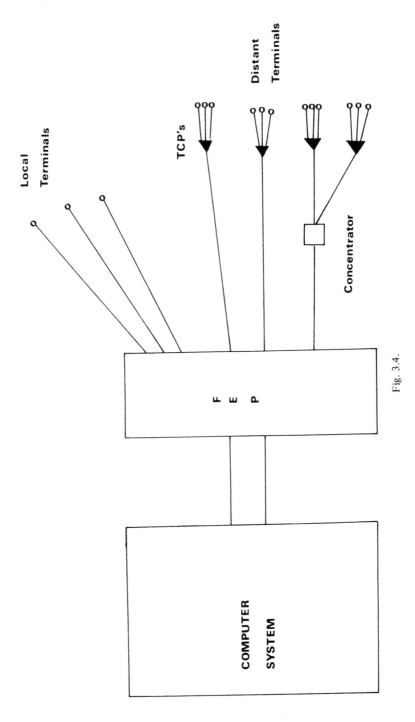

Fig. 3.4.

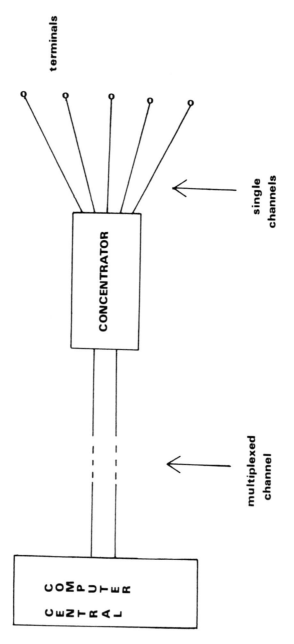

Fig. 3.5(a) — Use of a concentrator.

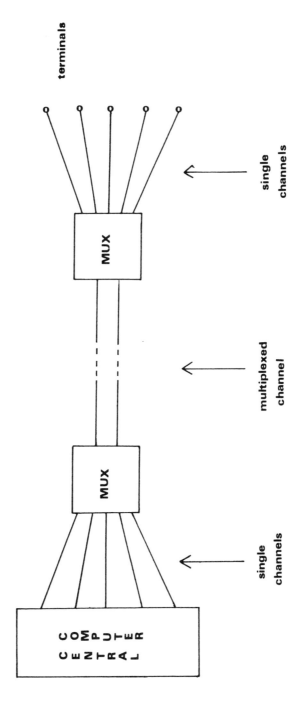

Fig. 3.5(b) – Use of a pair of multiplexors (MUX's).

firmware in multiplexors. The function of a multiplexor differs from that of a concentrator because they are used in a pair, one at each end of a transmission channel, making as many separate output channels as there were input channels. Concentrators are used singly, the central computer being used to perform the demultiplexing (see Fig. 3.5). The term 'multiplexor' is frequently contracted to MUX. As Fig. 3.5(b) shows, multiplexing is a transparent operation; the central computer is effectively connected by four direct lines to the remote terminals.

Multiplexors fall into two types according to the mechanisms by which they operate: Frequency Division Multiplexors (FDMs) and Time Division Multiplexors (TDMs). FDMs have long been used in the telephone and telex network but have largely been replaced by TDMs since the advent of high speed digital links on the trunk network.

3.5.1 Frequency Division Multiplexing

As described in Chapter 1 digital signals may be transmitted down a telephone line by the use of a modem which converts the two binary states into two different tones. If the band-width of the transmission channel is sufficient then more pairs of frequencies may be transmitted simultaneously. With the Bell 103A modem two 300 bps signals are sent on a voice grade telephone line to enable full duplex terminal operation: one end sends data using a pair of frequencies centred on 1170 Hz while the other end is centred on 2125 Hz. Fig. 3.6 shows how these frequencies fit into the passband of the telephone system which is 300-3000 Hz. 1070 Hz and 2025 Hz represent binary '0' and 1270 Hz and 2225 Hz binary '1' respective subchannels.

The shaded areas in Fig. 3.6 indicate the frequency and power spectrum transmitted when 300 bps data is sent through each subchannel. It is this wide spectrum of frequencies produced which prevents us from simply sending more frequency pairs or faster transmission rates down a channel of limited bandwidth.

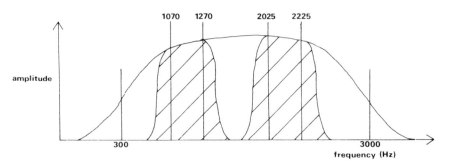

Fig. 3.6.

These other frequencies are produced as we are effectively frequency modulating a signal of 1170 Hz or 2125 Hz with a square wave having a peak frequency of 125 Hz (300 bps with every bit opposite in value to the previous) with a deviation of 100 Hz. Fourier analysis shows that a square wave can be decomposed to give very high frequency components which are responsible for the wide range of 'side-bands' produced.

The absolute limit on the rate at which data may be sent down a channel is given by Shannons Law:

$$C = W \log_2 \left(1 + \frac{S}{N}\right) \text{ bps.}$$

where C is data transmission rate in bps.
         W is band width in Hz.
         S is signal power.
         N is noise power assuming the noise is white or Gaussian.

If we assume the bandwidth of a telephone line to be 3000 Hz and the signal to noise power ratio to be 100 : 1 then

$$C = 3000 \log_2 \left(1 + \frac{100}{1}\right) = 19,963 \text{ bps}$$

This value is far greater than those found in practice: 9600 bps is typical for a good quality telephone line. This inferior performance occurs when the channel response is not constant over the whole bandwidth, the noise is not Gaussian and the coding used to send the data is not optimal.

Frequency division multiplexing was widely used for trunk telephone links in which many radio frequency carrier waves were each modulated by a single speech channel; the signals were then merged and transmitted through coaxial cable preventing leakage of the signals into free space. At the receiving end many radio detectors were coupled to the coaxial cable each tuned to the slightly different carrier frequencies thus reconstructing the many speech signals. Along the length of the coaxial cable repeaters were placed every few thousand metres amplifying the whole range of frequencies being transmitted. This technique was later translated to microwave and satellite links, but has now been largely superseded by digital transmission and the use of time division multiplexing.

3.5.2 Time Division Multiplexing

Time division multiplexing is a very simple concept. It can be considered as the action of two rotary switches acting sychronously so that only one of several input channels is connected to the transmission channel at any moment, and similarly for the output channel (see Fig. 3.7). If wiper 1 and wiper 2 are kept in step and the three contacts are at 120° angles to each other in a rotary switch, then as the wipers rotate the signal channel will be divided between the three subchannels.

Fig. 3.7.

In a digital multiplexing system the time at which each input line is sampled would need to be synchronised with the incoming data. Therefore a 1 bit buffer is used to store the latest binary value received on a line until that line is sampled. Often TDMs are flexible to allow for the varying requirements of different types of terminal equipment connected to it. For instance, a remote site may have an RJE terminal with fast line printer and card reader requiring a line speed of 9600 bps for full utilisation and two terminals of 1200 bps and 300 bps line speed. In this case for every sample of the 300 bps terminal taken, four would be taken from the 1200 bps terminal and thirty-two from the RJE terminal; thus a total of 37 X 300 bps is being sent. The line chosen to handle this would need to be a little faster than the 11,100 bps calculated, to allow for timing information to be sent to keep the two ends of the channel synchronised. For example, one popular TDM requires a 50 K bps line speed to send 48 K bps of user data.

3.5.3 Demand Multiplexing

Data transmitted to and from terminals is typically very sporadic, with no data being transmitted for the majority of the time. With FDMs and TDMs we described systems in which the subchannel capacities are fixed with no delays or congestion problems such as may occur using concentrators. The introduction of cheap microprocessors has lead to the development of multiplexors which apportion the channel, not according to preset proportions, but according to the demands of the various inputs. In this scheme a dormant channel is not allocated any slots in the transmitted bit stream, freeing space to be used by other heavily loaded subchannels. This technique is also called statistical multiplexing. Because each input line must have a buffer of considerable size associated with it to take full advantage of demand multiplexing, there may be delays between data arriving and space being found to send it — thus the congestion and delays of concentrators occur.

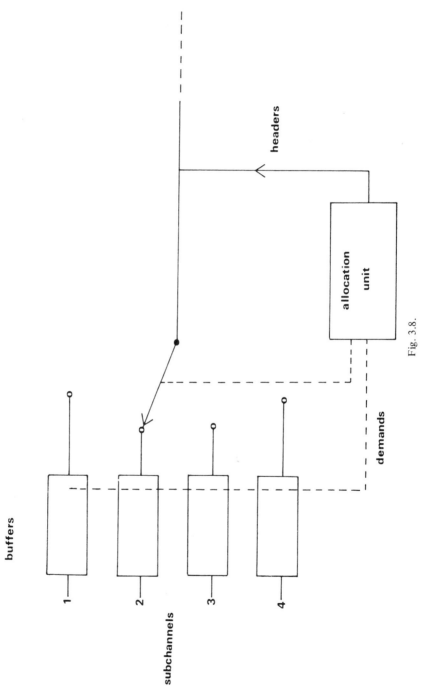

Fig. 3.8.

Demand multiplexors are implemented by replacing the switch which in a TDM 'rotates' uniformly sharing the channel between all the input lines with one which responds to data being placed in a line buffer. Each line is allocated an address which is sent as a header, followed by the data from the buffer so that on reception the data can be placed in the output buffer corresponding to the header contained in the address (see Fig. 3.8).

As buffers become larger and more lines are multiplexed in this way, we seem to return to a packet switching solution implemented in the hardware and firmware of multiplexors employing microcomputers as their logic elements.

3.6 BROADCAST DATA SYSTEMS

Previously we have considered data networks where several separate systems are interconnected by point to point links, either directly between them or via intermediate nodes. The one exception to this has been our consideration of multi-drop lines, which are an example of broadcast data systems, that is, systems in which all stations connected by some common medium can receive the emanations from all the other stations. The medium upon which the broadcast takes place may be high speed data lines; UHF or microwave radio; high bandwidth coaxial cable; or satellite links. Receiving data on a broadcast system is quite simple; each station listens to all transmissions, but only passes onto the data terminal equipment messages with the appropriate address in the message header. More difficult is the problem of controlling efficiently who may transmit on the channel at a given time, termed 'contention'. We could use a fixed scheme of division of a channel into timed slots, effectively time division multiplexing, but Time Division Multiple Access (TDMA) is inefficient when the channels are sporadically used. We need a system analogous to the demand multiplexing we encountered earlier. The problems are slightly different for satellite channels as opposed to radio or cable systems due to the long delays encountered. In the case of a geostationary satellite the journeys of the radio signals from earth to satellite and back takes about 270 milliseconds. In cable or terrestrial radio systems the propagation times are extremely short. A possible mechanism for solving the contention problem is to listen to the transmission medium before commencing transmission; clashes will only occur if two or more stations start to transmit simultaneously or very close to it. This listen-before-transmit scheme is not possible for satellite systems, which generally operate with separate up-channel and down-channel frequencies. The transmitting earth stations will not be able to hear that a clash has occurred by listening to the down-channel until about 270 milliseconds after the transmission. Satellite links are usually so reliable that if the sending earth station is able to hear a correct relay of the packet sent when it is retransmitted by the satellite, it is highly probable that the destination earth station will also receive the data correctly. To ensure absolute integrity of the data some sort of end-to-end protocol is added to give acknowledgement of correctly received data packets. The solutions to the contention problem depend partly on the nature of the communications medium used, so we shall consider separately UHF radio, cable, and satellite systems.

3.6.1 UHF Radio Systems

One of the first UHF radio systems for data transmission was built by the University of Hawaii in 1970 to provide terminal access to outlying groups of users in an area where telephone communications were poor. The system called ALOHA utilises two UHF channels; one for computer to user, the other for user to computer transmission. The system provides a wireless network for accessing a central system; user to user communications is only supported via the central computer. Packets of data are sent at 9600 bps with the format: header – 4 bytes, header checksum – 2 bytes, data up to 80 bytes, and data checksum – 2 bytes. The header contains the address of the desination terminal for packets sent from the central station, or the originating terminal for data sent to it. Obviously there is no problem with terminal directed traffic; the central station transmits packets sent to it from the central computer in turn, and the various receiving stations recognise and act only on those packets with the correct address in the header. Whenever a remote terminal has data to send, it transmits it immediately. Whenever the central station receives a packet correctly it sends an acknowledgement packet. If this is not recieved by a terminal within a time-out period, the terminal resends the packet after a random delay. Apart from possible noise swamping the terminal stations packet, the most likely cause for packet corruption is a collision occurring as two terminals transmit simultaneously, causing the central station to receive garbage. The random delay is introduced to ensure that the collision does not simply repeat itself by both terminals timing out and retransmitting again simultaneously. This scheme is called 'pure ALOHA'; it has been shown that at best only 18.4% of the channel bandwidth is used. This low maximum throughput of pure ALOHA is due to the fairly high probability of clashes occurring during the transmission of a packet which takes 73 milliseconds to transmit. The efficiency can be doubled by introducing timeslots at intervals of time equal to the packet transmission time – 73 milliseconds in this case. A terminal is only allowed to start a packet transmission exactly at the start of one of these slots. This increase in efficiency occurs because the maximum duration of a corruption is now one packet's duration, because the terminals are bound to start transmission simultaneously. In pure ALOHA almost two packets duration may be corrupted by a collision if the last bit of one packet collides with the first bit of another. This modification is known as 'slotted ALOHA'. Another way of improving efficiency is by stations listening to the transmit channel before themselves transmitting – if they hear another station transmitting they defer starting their own for a random period. If the deferred period was not random, several stations might all start transmitting as soon as another stopped. This mode of operation is called carrier sense multiple access (CSMA). This method cannot prevent exactly simultaneously transmission from clashing, nor can it cope if stations are hidden from each other, either by distance or terrain.

3.6.2 Cable Systems

Cable systems for packet broadcast share some of the characteristics of UHF radio systems: the signals can either be sent as baseband digital signals, that is, the high and low voltages representing binary ones and zeros are directly fed into the cable; or a carrier signal can be modulated in some way to carry the information. Unlike the radio systems, all stations connected to a cable can hear each others transmissions; there is no master receiver which can hear all remote stations and send acknowledgements of correct reception of packets. Because of this a modification to the CSMA policy described previously can be made: Listen While Talk (LWT). Not only does the station listen to the cable before starting transmission in order to ensure no other transmissions are taking place, but is also listens to the cable during its transmission. This LWT mode permits a station to detect when a transmission sent by itself has been corrupted — it has only to compare each bit it sends with each it receives. If a collision is detected then both the stations stop immediately and wait for a random period before retrying the transmission. When any station detects a collision it transmits a burst of random data to ensure that the other stations also detect it. Because the stations themselves detect collisions and stop immediately, the throughput of the system can be greater than in the radio situation where the stations only realise a collision has occurred by not receiving an acknowledgement from the central station before the time-out period has elapsed. Unless a very high degree of data integrity is required, no end-to-end error detecting/correcting protocol is required: this error free property is due to the cable not being subject to external noise; and the length such that with the given transmitter/receivers the signal should be strong enough at all points to be detected without error. Thus, if the transmitting station is able to receive its own transmission without any corruption, then so should any other station on the cable.

The dominant cable system in use is the Ethernet developed by Xerox: the above description is based on that used in Ethernet. The sort of communications systems suited to this type of approach are local area networks, in which are connected various small machines, and possibly large mainframe computers within a limited physical area, of perhaps one kilometre. Such a system might interconnect word processors to provide electronic mail in an organisation's offices, or to connect data from monitoring points in a manufacturing process.

Another widely mentioned cable system is the Cambridge Ring, developed at Cambridge University Computer Laboratory. This is not a broadcast system but we describe it here for the sake of completeness. The Cambridge Ring consists of a complete loop of cable which leaves from and returns to a ring control station. The remote stations are connected to the ring in a similar way; whereas in Ethernet, stations inject their signals onto a cable which passes by them. In a Cambridge Ring each station is in series with the cable; it is an active device at all times it receives a stream of bits on one side, retransmitting them on the other. As the stream of bits passes through the receiver/transmitter individual packets are recognised, their addresses can be examined and the data accepted if the address is that of the receiver/transmitter station it is passing through. If the packet is accepted it is marked on the outgoing side of the station as empty. A station with data to transmit waits for an empty packet to arrive and fills it with the data and destination address. The control station is used to remove corrupted packets or packets which have circulated several times without being accepted by the destination, thus preventing the infinite circulation of packets addressed to non-existent or busy stations. Packets are circulated at a rate of several hundred thousand per second, so data transfer rates can be very high. The contention problem is simply solved by having the remote stations wait for an empty packet to arrive. The speeds of sending and receiving the data are such that Cambridge Rings can be quite critical to set up correctly; if either the control station or any of the remote stations becomes faulty, the ring cannot operate; if they are powered off they must be bypassed.

3.6.3 Satellite Systems

When satellite systems are used to provide multi-access broadcast data facilities, they combine some of the properties of both terrestrial radio and cable systems. Like terrestrial radio systems they operate in transponder mode, that is, they receive data on the frequency in multi-access mode, and retransmit it on another frequency in broadcast mode. They share with cable systems the property whereby if the transmitting groundstation correctly receives the transponded version of its packet, the chances are very high that the destination also received it correctly. The receiver in each groundstation receives all packets broadcast by the satellite, but only passes on those packets addressed to itself to the data terminal equipment. As the ground stations cannot directly hear one anothers transmissions, contention for the channel cannot be controlled by carrier sense multiple access, so either pure or slotted ALOHA, or some other method may be used. The particular characteristic of satellite circuits is the long path used in the link, because in order to appear at a fixed point above the earth they must orbit at 36000 Km above the equator. The round trip of twice this distance takes 240-270 milliseconds at the speed of light, depending on whether the satellite is directly overhead or near the horizon. If we use an ALOHA scheme it will be up to 270 milliseconds before we know if a collision has occurred, and at best we only make use of 36.8% of the available capacity of the expensive satellite channel. A more efficient way to use the available capacity is through a scheme of slot reservations, in which a groundstation with data to send can make a reservation in a special reservation slot for a future information slot.

This method is similar to demand multiplexing in concept: as in slotted ALOHA the system operates synchronously, that is, the groundstations may only transmit fixed length packets starting at fixed time intervals. Periodically special slots called reservation slots are transmitted: each reservation slot is divided into n minislots, where n is the number of groundstations using the channel. A groundstation wishing to reserve a future slot for transmission must transmit a request during the minislot allocated to it. When the reservations slot is returned to earth 270 milliseconds later, all the groundstations can see which other groundstations have requested information slots. By giving each groundstation a fixed priority and a common algorithm based on these fixed priorities, each groundstation can calculate which subsequent information slots it may use, with no risk of collision if all groundstations keep to the rules. Thus, except for the overhead of periodic reservation slots, this system can provide full channel ultilisation. This system developed by Hwa is called Conflict Free Multiaccess (CFMA).

3.7 DIAGNOSTIC AIDS

When a communications system is in operation any problems arising need to be solved with minimal disturbance to the users. How much disturbance the users will tolerate depends on the nature of the user; whether he is paying for the facility, and the nature of the communications he is using. If the user is inter-actively accessing a remote computer via a terminal control processor any break will be of great irritation. If the network is only used for batch transactions, such as remotely listing output or transferring files, the users may not notice a short break. Essentially therefore, tools we use to diagnose problems need to be transparent as far as possible, and either built in or easily slotted in to cause minimal interruption when they are brought into service. This generalisation applies equally to software and hardware diagnostic aids.

Starting at the lowest level we need some way of testing that the basic hardware of a communications link is functioning. Very often a leased line will have a telephone which can be switched into circuit, in place of the modem, thus enabling the operator of a computer at one end of a link to call and speak to the operator at the remote end; if a two-way conversation is possible then the basic telephone link is functioning satisfactorily. Use of the speech facility over a leased data link will however stop any data from being sent, and in the case of a full digital telephone system the speech facility may not be provided. Most modems will have either a light or meter to indicate that a carrier is being detected by the modem, emanating from the remote modem. If both ends show carrier detect on them the telephone link is probably functioning.

The next convenient place to observe a data link is at the interface between the computer and the modem: At this point a tool showing the status of the various lines is useful, on a V.24 interface for example. At the simplest level we have the 'lights box' in which the state of each V.24 line is shown, on or off, by a light. In more sophisticated versions it is possible to alter the state of various lines to either simulate or correct fault conditions. Another elaboration is in providing a patch panel whereby lines can be interconnected, for example to try a null modem configuration. If the interface appears to be correct, then the problem may be faulty handling of the protocol. A lights box may be able to tell us if data is being sent or received, as the appropriate light will flicker on as the data passes through, but it cannot tell if the data is sensible. For this we need a line-monitor or data-scope. This device, like the lights box operates transparently: in essence it consists of two receivers; one for each direction, and a visual display unit. The receivers will be programmable to use various synchronising characters; different lengths of characters; and display different character codes. Using a line monitor it is possible to examine exactly what data is being sent; this is very useful when developing communications software. Line monitors are often enhanced by the addition of a printer and magnetic tape recorder so that the data flow can be analysed at leisure. The software in the line monitor may also allow the picture to be frozen on command, or upon receipt of a determined sequence of characters, or to count various occurrences or time intervals between events. At the peak of complexity they may be able to generate packets of data themselves in response to particular events.

Software as complex as communications programs should be designed with debugging as an important priority. In situations where new software is being written to connect a new host to a network, the network can provide some helpful facilities. Aids often found in packet switched networks include sinks, where a node accepts packets for a dummy destination and throws them away, and echoes, at which the source and destination addresses in a packet are reversed so the packet returns to its origin. In networks where dynamic routing is used the tracer can be helpful, this special packet causes a packet to be returned to the source of the tracer at each node it visits, indicating the route that each one takes. This facility is of use to a network engineer, rather than an individual host on a network. The software in the switching nodes will be programmed to collect statistics on traffic flows and queue during operation; these are periodically sent to a network diagnostic centre which in turn may be alerted to problems by analysis of the statistics gathered.

CHAPTER 4

Implementation

4.1 INTRODUCTION TO REAL MACHINES

Although software is currently being written increasingly in high-level languages, even for applications previously identified as normally needing the efficiency and directness of assembler language coding, the systems we will discuss will be at the machine instruction level. This is done for two reasons: it is easier to see the exact actions of the samples given at the bit level; and also because most communications programs at their lowest level are still written in an assembler language. Computers are still becoming cheaper and faster but it is a waste of expensive resources to inefficiently implement routines which will be called frequently. If, for example, we are using simple communications interfaces which have only a single character buffer needing to be emptied before the next character has been received, operating at a medium speed such as 9600 bps, we shall need to remove 1200 cps from it, assuming 8 bit characters are used. If a computer has five such links operating, then the code to remove the characters from the interfaces will be executed 6000 times per second. Obviously for code executed as often as this it is essential to make it as efficient as possible so that the computer can actually process usefully the information it receives. This level of activity is not rare and can with care be implemented on fairly small minicomputers. As the frequency of invocation of routines decreases it becomes more reasonable to use a suitable high-level language; even so, comparatively few languages can provide the sort of operations needed to perform such things as parity checking or block check character calculation. There seems little point in struggling to perform an 'exclusive or' operation in Fortran if the instruction repertoire of the computer possesses the instruction.

4.2 EXAMPLES USING PDP11

One of the most widely used minicomputers very often found in communications applications is the Digital Equipment Corporation's PDP11. Although introduced in the early 1970s, the instruction set has been retained in subsequent generations of hardware so that there exists a range of machines from the PDP11/03 (often used with 16-24 K bytes of memory in dedicated applications such as operating as a terminal control processor) to the PDP11/70 which can be used as a multi-access time sharing system with several mega-bytes of storage and large discs etc. We will discuss techniques for the use of both the small dedicated systems requiring a simple executive to run one dedicated task, and the use of large systems with an operating system supplied by the manufacturer. In describing the systems we will not use specific communications devices as these would become rapidly obsolete and also prevent us from understanding the general principles by involving us with their individual foibles, instead we will invent representative examples.

4.2.1 Outline Architecture of the PDP11

The PDP11 is a computer using 16 bit words divided into two 8 bit bytes. There are instructions which can operate on either the word or byte as their addressable unit. We will not here describe in detail the instruction set; comments will be included in any program sections given to enable them to be understood. Many operations have two variants, either for word or byte operations; the mnemonics for the byte oriented version are usually terminated by 'B', for example, MOV is used to move a word from a source to destination, MOVB to move a byte. Most operations have one or two operands; either simply a destination, or a source and destination for the operation, for example, MOV uses a source and a destination to indicate what is to be moved to where, while CLR, (the clear operation) only requires a destination to indicate the location in which zero should be stored. The source and destination referenced in an instruction may either be one of the registers or a memory location. There are eight registers, six of which are general purpose – R0–R5; R6 is used to point to the next free element of a stack, and R7 is used as the program counter, that is, it points to the next instruction to be executed. R6 and R7 are normally referred to as SP and PC respectively to indicate their functions. The stack can be used for temporary storage of variables or register contents by explicitly moving data to it, or it can be used implicitly when calling a subroutine, for example, when the return address is placed on the stack. From the communications point of view the method of accessing peripheral devices such as synchronous communications interfaces and such like is of greater interest than simply describing the instruction set which is well known and widely documented.

Unlike many systems the PDP11 does not include IN or OUT operations in its instruction repertoire in order to communicate with the outside world. For internal communications the system uses a word-wide parallel bus to connect CPU, memory and peripheral devices. Because anything connected to the bus is only accessed by giving its address, it makes no difference at any point if the address given is interpreted to mean a memory location or the buffer built into a peripheral device. By convention the physical peripherals are given addresses much higher than any real memory in use in the system. Each physical device will have at least two memory locations associated with it, usually contiguous; one for the data the device has received or is to send, and another to either indicate or alter the status of the device, called the 'status register'. Some devices which perform complicated activities may use several status registers. For slow to medium speed devices such as a synchronous line interface working at 9600 bps the data is received or transmitted a byte at a time and the processor is informed when the buffer needs to be served, either because a character has been received or sent. The processor is informed by the occurrence of an 'interrupt'. An interrupt is analogous to a subroutine call which occurs not because a program has requested it but because an external event has occurred. Like a subroutine call the current program counter is stored on the stack so that whatever task was being executed can be resumed when the event has been dealt with.

There are two ways in which interrupts can be handled on a computer, depending on the degree of sophistication of the hardware. The simplest method is to cause an interrupt to initiate a program starting at a fixed place in memory which checks the status register of each device in the system to find out which one caused the interrupt and then perform whatever action is required. A more complex solution to find the source of an interrupt is to use hardware which will 'vector' interrupts. In this scheme the peripheral device which requested the interrupt also supplies an address to the processor at which it should start execution of the interrupt handling routine. In this way no time needs to be spent testing the status of all the devices in the system to find the source of the interrupt as each device causes the processor to jump to its own device handling routine. This vectored interrupt mechanism is used on the PDP11. The vector address to be jumped to when a device requests an interrupt is set by altering small switches on the interface board to the binary representation of the address required. For a device consisting of a receiver and transmitter which are two logically separate parts, two interrupt locations will be used to specify which part of the device the interrupt came from. We will now describe some communications devices and the interface they present to the programmer.

4.2.2 Interfaces Using Interrupts — An Asynchronous Serial Example

This type of interface may be used to drive either local terminals connected by a null modem or remote terminals connected by a real modem and a telephone line. It will receive and transmit data at normal terminal speeds between 110 and 9600 bps. Four 16 bit registers are provided by the interface; a status and data buffer register for both the receiver and transmitter. Two interrupt locations are used, one for the receiver and one for the transmitter. The receiver interrupt location is used to signal two possible situations which must be tested by the interrupt routine whenever it is invoked — for Receive Done, indicating a character has been received, and data-set status change, caused by a change in status of one of the modem control lines. The functions of the four registers will now be described.

Receiver Status Register Bit Assignment

Dataset Status Change (read only) — This bit is set if a change in state of any of the bits Carrier Detect, Clear To Send, Ring Indicator occurs. If the Dataset Interrupt Enable bit is set, an interrupt to the receive vector address will also occur.

Carrier Detect (read only) — This bit reflects the state of the modem line of the same name. The set state indicates carrier is present.

Clear To Send (read only) — This follows the state of the modem line indicating when set that the modem is capable of sending data,

Ring Indicator (read only) — This is set on when the modem's ring indicator line is set. It only causes Dataset State Change to be set or the receiver interrupt to occur when the off to on transition occurs, thus only one interrupt per ring occurs.

Receiver Active (read only) — This bit is set on as soon as a valid start bit is detected on the received data line. It remains on until Receiver Done is set when the complete character has been received.

Receiver Done (read only) — This bit is set on when a complete character has been received and transferred to the receiver buffer register. If the Receiver Interrupt Enable bit is set on an interrupt to the receiver interrupt vector occurs. This bit is cleared when the character is read from the receiver buffer register.

Receiver Interrupt Enable (read/write) — When set this bit causes an interrupt to occur whenever the Receiver Done bit is set.

Dataset Interrupt Enable (read/write) — When set this bit causes an interrupt to occur whenever the Dataset Status Change bit is set.

Request To Send (read/write) — The modem control line of the same name follows the state of this line, it must be set on before transmission can occur.

Data Terminal Ready (read/write) — This bit controls the modem line of the same name in order to answer and maintain calls on the dial-up telephone system.

It will be noticed that not all sixteen bits have been used in this typical receiver status register. Frequently several bits are left free for future enhancements while others are used to switch on maintenance mode diagnostic facilities not normally used other than by engineer's test programs.

Receiver Buffer Register Bit Assignments

Error (read only) — This bit is set if either of the bits Overrun or Framing Error are set.

Overrun (read only) — This bit is set if a new character has been received before the previous one has been read from the receiver buffer data byte.

Framing Error (read only) — This bit is set if a stop bit is not found when expected. This may indicate that the receiver data line has become disconnected or there is excessive distortion of the received characters bit timings.

The latest character to be received is placed in the lower byte of the register from where it may be read.

Transmitter Status Register Bit Assignments

Transmitter Ready (read only) — This bit is set whenever the transmitter is able to accept a new character for sending it. It is cleared when a data byte is placed in the transmitter buffer register. If Transmitter Interrupt Enable is set then an interrupt to the transmitter vector address occurs when the bit is set.

Transmitter Interrupt Enable (read/write) — When this bit is set an interrupt is generated whenever Transmitter Ready is set.

The transmitter data buffer register only uses the lower byte into which data to be transmitted should be placed.

The bits assigned in these sixteen bit registers can be written to or read from using any instruction able to access memory. The registers can be given symbolic names in PDP11 assembler using the .ASECT directive. This generates code to be loaded at an absolute physical address rather than relocated to whatever address is chosen when the code is loaded, for example:

```
        .ASECT  777560      ; Octal Address of first register
RXSR:  .WORD   0           ; Receiver Status Register
RBUF:  .WORD   0           ; Receiver Data Buffer
TXSR:  .WORD   0           ; Transmitter Status Register
TBUF:  .WORD   0           ; Transmitter Data Buffer
```

To read a character from the receiver data buffer into a register for processing we could use the instruction:

```
MOVB  RBUF,R1
```

We can also use the .ASECT directive to set up the interrupt vector locations. Each interrupt vector consists of two locations; these two locations are placed into the 'program counter' and 'program status' registers respectively, the old values being placed on the stack so that the interrupted task can be resumed when the interrupt has been serviced, for example:

```
.ASECT   40              ; Address of lower vector
.WORD    RINT            ; Address of receiver interrupt routine
.WORD    PRIST           ; Privileged status for interrupt routine
.WORD    TINT            ; Address of transmitter interrupt routine
.WORD    PRIST           ; Privileged status for interrupt routine
```

Now follows an example of the use of the transmitter section of an asynchronous line driver to print a string of characters terminated by a zero byte on a local terminal. The program will be in two parts; the first to set up the transmitter into a state in which it is ready for sending, the second to handle the interrupts caused as each character is sent, called 'XMIT' and 'TINT' respectively. XMIT should be called with register 0 containing the address of the string to be sent, for example:

```
STRING: .ASCII /THE∇QUICK∇BROWN∇FOX/
        .BYTE  CR,LF,0          ; Carriage return and line feed
```

The calling sequence for XMIT is thus:

```
MOV  #STRING,R0              ; Get address of string
CALL  XMIT
```

The XMIT routine will set the modem control line Data Terminal Ready to the on state. Data will be sent immediately as it is assumed that the terminal is connected locally and we do not have to assert Request To Send and wait for Clear To Send to be set by a modem.

```
TIEBIT  = bit pattern for Transmitter Interrupt Enable in TXSR
DTRBIT = bit pattern to set Data Terminal Ready on in RXSR

XMIT:    BIS  #DTRBIT,RXSR    ; Assert DTR
         BIS  #TIEBIT,TXSR    ; Enable transmitter interrupts
         MOVB (R0),RBUF       ; Send first character
         INC R0               ; Point at next
         MOV  R0,XPTR         ; Save pointer
         RETURN               ; Return to main program

XPTR:    .WORD 0              ; Space for pointer

TINT:    MOV  R0,-(SP)        ; Save R0 on stack
         MOV  XPTR,R0         ; Get pointer
         TSTB (R0)            ; Hit 0 at end of string yet?
         BZ  ALLX             ; Exit if true
```

```
                MOVB (R0),TBUF          ; Send next character
                INC  XPTR               ; Point at next

        ALLX:   MOV  (SP)+,R0           ; Restore old value of R0
                RTI                     ; Return from interrupt
```

Assembler programs for the PDP11 are written with four fields: label, operator, operand and comment fields. The operand field may contain one or two operands depending on the type of operation. The BIS operation causes the bits set on in the first operand to be set in the second operand, that is, a logical 'or' is performed. The # sign is used to indicate that the symbolic names being used should yield their actual values and not point at memory. If for example TIEBIT was set to 200_8 the bit pattern to be logically 'or'd' with the second operand would be: 0000000010000000, and not the contents of memory location 200_8. It was specified that R0 (register 0) would contain the address of the start of the string to be sent. The operand (R0) causes the processor to use the value stored in R0 to obtain the address of the character to be moved in the MOVB instruction, rather than moving the actual value in the register. The INC operation causes one to be added to the value of the operand. The value of R0 is then stored in a separate memory location XPTR as we should not expect the calling program to preserve the contents of R0 until some time in the future when the string has been sent.

As soon as each character has been removed from the transmitter buffer to the internal shift register in the device an interrupt occurs requesting new data to be placed in the buffer. The routine named TINT responds to these interrupts by sending the next character unless there are no more to send, in which case it simply exits and the sending process ends. In practice the program which initiated the transmission would want to know that the string had been sent, perhaps so that it could send another. This could be done by a variety of means, perhaps simplest would be to allocate another memory location to act as a flag to indicate when transmission was finished. When the transmitter interrupt routine detects the zero byte terminating the string it could place a known value in this flag location. Because TINT will be entered during the execution of other programs whenever an interrupt occurs, it cannot alter the registers without causing the interrupted program to malfunction when it is resumed. If it uses any registers it must therefore save the old value and restore it when the routine is exited. On some computers this problem is bypassed by using a special set of registers when in interrupt mode which are not accessible from ordinary processes. In this example we use one register whose original value is saved on the machine stack by the operation: MOV R0,-(SP). This single operation causes the value of the stack pointer to be decremented (the stack grows downwards in store in the PDP11) and the value of R0 to be stored at the address pointed to by the stack pointer. The value in XPTR, which points at the next character to be sent is then moved to R0. The TSTB operation is used to set the condition codes which are tested by the conditional branch instructions; it contains bits to indicate whether the result of each operation was positive, negative or zero. If the byte pointed at by R0 contains zero, to indicate the end of the string, the zero bit of the condition code will be set and the BZ (branch if zero) operation will cause the program to jump to the label ALLX, indicating that the complete string has been sent. If the byte was non-zero its value is moved to TBUF, the transmitter buffer from where it will be sent. The value in XPTR which points at the character just placed in the transmitter buffer is then incremented by one, thus pointing at the next character to be sent when the interrupt routine is next entered. To resume the interrupted process the old value of R0 is restored and the RTI returns the value of the program counter and program status registers to their values before the interrupt occurred.

Creating a program to receive data is very similar in that a small piece of code would be executed to initiate the read and from then on execution would be started at an interrupt routine to handle each incoming character.

This interrupt-driven input/output is more efficient than the crude alternative in which, after each byte of data is received or transmitted, the program sits in a small loop checking the status of the device's Ready bit. This polling operation to test for the completion of operations does not leave the machine free to perform any other activities while waiting for the next data byte. There are very few applications, even using dedicated communications computers, when we can afford to waste so much processor time.

4.2.3 Interfaces Using Direct Memory Access – A Synchronous Serial Example

To program a synchronous interface is quite a similar process to an asynchronous one. However, there are a few differences due to the different mode of transmission used. Before the receiver can receive any data it must be in a synchronised state so that it can recognise the boundaries of the characters from the continuous stream of bits it receives. As many different synchronising characters are used in different systems, space is usually found in a status register to contain a synchronising character from the driving program. It is the responsibility of the program controlling the transmitter to send several synchronising characters at the start of each transmission. Once transmission has commenced the transmitter must receive characters from the program to send within the time taken to send one character at whatever line speed is used. 'Underrun' is said to occur if the transmitter has no data to send at the appropriate time; it is a serious error which will cause loss of synchonisation at the receiver. For line speeds of up to about 9.6 K bps the interrupt per character interface to the program is satisfactory, causing up to 1200 interrupts per second. If several such interfaces are to be supported, or faster line speeds are required then the burden on the computer system of handling an interrupt per character may be too much. As an alternative to interrupt per character devices, more complex versions are available which are able to receive or transmit data directly from buffers in the main store of the computer. These more complex interfaces can be obtained to transfer data synchronously at up to 1M bps. This rate of data transfer is obviously not obtainable with interrupt per character devices as it implies 125000 interrupts per second to be handled, many small computers can only manage that number of instructions per second and so could obviously not cope. Even on these slow machines the internal rate of data transfer is in excess of 1M bps so that a 1M bps data transfer to or from a communications interface can occur simultaneously with normal operation of the processor. Using this DMA (direct memory access) mode of operation the processor is only interrupted after a complete message has been sent or received. The operation of the receiver is complicated by not knowing in advance how many characters to expect. This means we do not know how big a buffer we need to supply to receive the incoming data, and we do not know when the incoming data ends. We overcome the first problem by defining in the protocol used on the data link the maximum message length and assigning buffers of this length. The latter problem is dealt with by arranging for a special character to be sent at the end of each message. When the hardware of the interface recognises the special 'end-of-message' character, it causes a 'receive-done' interrupt to inform the control program that a complete message has been received. Probably there will be several characters which can end a message and the device may provide either software commands or hardware options which can be altered by changing links on the printed circuit board on which the interface is built. A typical interface of this type will be accessed by two sets of registers, one for the receiver and one for the transmitter. Each set will have the normal status and control register as in the interrupt driven interface, and also address and character count registers. The control and status registers enable the modem control lines to be either set or tested and also control the enabling or disabling of interrupts generated by the device. If interrupts are enabled they will only occur after a complete message has been either sent or received. The address register is used to indicate to the device where it should place the characters it receives, or where the characters to be sent are located. The character count register contains the number of characters received or to be sent. Once the addresses have been set of the buffer to be used and for the transmitter character count, the transfer is initiated by setting either Receive Go or Transmitter Go in the appropriate control register. The errors which may occur with a DMA type transfer are slightly different to those with simple byte at a time transfers. The interface accesses memory directly using successive addresses starting at the address contained in the address register. It is possible that at some stage before the transfer is completed that the address either may not exist or may not be legally accessible due to the operation of some memory protection hardware in a multi-tasking system. This type of error will cause an error interrupt to occur if error interrupts are enabled, or will set an error flag. The equivalent of the error condition termed 'underrun' for transmitting or 'overrun' on receiving with character at a time interfaces can still occur but are termed 'latency' errors. These latency errors can only occur if the bus upon which data is transferred between peripherals, memory, and the central processor is overloaded. This situation should not occur unless the interface is being run at a speed in excess of that of the bus, or too many devices are competing for the bus. Thus the occurrence of latency errors implies that the computer system is not sufficiently powerful to handle the load placed upon it.

The use of DMA interfaces was until recently reserved for applications demanding very high throughput as they were much more expensive than character interrupt devices. The reduction in the cost of hardware has now made them attractive in non-critical situations simply to allow the central processor to concentrate on useful work for users. It is possible to obtain DMA interfaces supporting sixteen asynchronous lines for connection to terminals. This type of device will use DMA for transmission of messages out, with a set of sixteen pairs of address and character count registers. For reception DMA is not used as different programs require different terminators, and for editing purposes may want to examine each character as it is received. Also terminals do not create a large load for input as human operators do not type very fast. Nevertheless a system is often used to reduce the overhead of handling many slow connections. Rather than interrupt the processor each time a character is received the characters are stored in a memory device in the interface called a 'silo'. This is effectively a hardware-implemented queue using first-in, first-out operation. The head of this queue is the receive data buffer. Associated with the silo is a register containing an alarm value. When the number of characters in the silo reaches this value a receiver interrupt occurs. If this value is set to 1 the interface behaves exactly as a simple interrupt per character device. If the alarm is set for say 32 for a 64 character silo capacity, the interrupt routine when it is invoked reads in a fast loop until the status register indicates that the silo has been emptied. Each entry in the silo is sixteen bits wide, allowing for an 8 bit character, a 4 bit number to indicate which of the lines (0–15) it was received on, and four bits of status information.

Increasingly complex interfaces are now available which not only use DMA transfers but also can create or check parity bits on characters and also block check or cyclic check characters. This level of sophistication is exceeded in some devices which can handle a complete protocol. It is necessary only to queue buffers to be either sent or received containing or yielding the message alone with no control characters to interpret or check sums to evaluate. These are presently only available for manufacturer-specific protocols but it seems likely that they will soon be available to deal with X.25 to level three.

In the preceding description of both interrupt-driven and DMA devices no type names have been specified. As the technology is developing rapidly, obsolesence is also rapid, hence readers are referred to the latest product description issued by the manufacturers.

4.3 OPERATING SYSTEMS FOR COMMUNICATIONS

4.3.1 Executive Requirements for a Dedicated System

The essential requirements for an operating system or executive under which communications programs are to run is that it provides a facility for handling external events rapidly. This is usually called a 'real time facility'. The exact nature and complexity of the system will depend on whether it is only controlling a single dedicated task, such as a remote job entry computer, or terminal control processor, or whether it is a general purpose system able to run users' tasks as well as communicating with remote devices. It is becoming increasingly popular to merge functions previously kept separate, such as building a PAD facility into the operating system so that terminals directly connected to a computer can either use its local facilities, or call a remote computer on an X.25 network via the built in PAD.

Even if the computer is being used for a single dedicated function it will still be necessary to be able to schedule several tasks simultaneously competing for the central processor. This is because even the simplest system will still have several interrupting peripheral devices which need to be serviced within a short time of the interrupt being flagged. It is not generally possible then to completely process the interrupt and handle whatever data has been transferred within the interrupt handling routine. When an interrupt routine is executing, other interrupts are disabled until the routine is complete, thus if the processing of data was performed in the interrupt routine it is likely that data overruns or underruns would occur on other peripheral devices. To ensure that one task does not hog the processor because its high processing requirements a clock is normally incorporated into the system so that an interrupt occurs on every tick. Thus even if the peripherals are inactive there is still the chance to reallocate the processor to some other task with work to do. The clocks used are normally simple devices deriving their timing from the frequency of the a.c. power supply, that is, 50 Hz in Europe or 60 Hz in USA. A simple dedicated RJE system with card-reader, line-printer, console, clock and synchronous full duplex line interface might have software composed of seven logically distinct tasks. These tasks will be combined with the executive to be used and probably loaded as a binary card pack through the card reader. The facilities required of an executive program for this type of system are: ability to share the processor among several competing tasks; to handle interrupts from peripheral devices and wake up tasks which are suspended awaiting some external event; and to pass data from one task to another. In this system each of the seven tasks is associated with a peripheral and a queue of requests for that task. It may place requests for actions in the queues of other tasks. These queues will grow and shrink dynamically and space will also be required dynamically to multiple buffer input. This control of dynamic storage may also usefully form part of the executive, although it is not essential. Multiple buffering of input is performed to allow for transient speed discrepancies between different devices. If, for example, a number of very short lines of data destined for the line printer are received, the printer may not be able to keep up, whereas when long lines are received the printer may be kept waiting for the next line to be received by the interface. As long as the overall rate of transmission on the data line does not exceed the capacity of the line printer these transient differences in speed can be evened out without having to tell the source of the data to pause when the data acceptor cannot keep up. In outline the seven tasks will function as follows:

Line Interface Receiver will permanently have several buffers available to pass to the executive interrupt handler for the receiver. It will suspend itself awaiting the arrival of a complete message at which time the executive will reactivate it. When a message has been received a new buffer will be queued for the receiver interface and the contents of the received data analysed. If the message contains data for the line printer or the console, this data will be moved to a buffer which is then sent to the appropriate queue for the device to be printed or displayed. The message might contain information of a supervisory nature, such as requesting the card reader to start, in which case a special message will be sent to the card reader queue.

Line Interface Transmitter will suspend itself awaiting buffers to be placed in its queue. When a buffer is queued for it, the executive will wake it. The task will then arrange the data into a suitable form of transmission in order to conform with the protocol rules for the link and send the buffer to the executive transmitter handling routine. The task will then be suspended until the transmission is complete and the next data buffer to be sent is either dequeued if it exists, or the task suspends itself awaiting its arrival.

Clock – Most protocols specify that even if no data is being sent, both ends of a link should periodically send a null packet to the other to indicate that the link and both computers are still functioning. Typical intervals might be every 1 to 5 seconds. Each time the line interfaces either receive or transmit data over the link they queue a message to the clock to indicate they have done so. The clock task suspends itself awaiting some interval of time to elapse at which point it will be reactivated for example after 50 ticks of the real time clock, that is, 1 second. When reactivated the clock queue is checked to see if an entry from both the receiver and transmitter are present. If there are no buffers queued by the transmitter then an 'idle' message is queued for it. If no buffer is queued by the receiver then the remote computer or data link have probably failed; a message will be queued for console output to indicate this to the operator and also for the card reader to stop as no more data can be transmitted until the remote system is functioning again.

Card Reader – This task will be suspended awaiting a buffer to be added to its queue requesting it to start reading. When reading has been initiated buffers are obtained and passed to the executive card reader interface handler. As each card is read the buffer containing the data is placed into the line interface queue to await transmission. As the line interface transmitter accepts buffers from its input queue it queues messages for the card reader to indicate acceptance. By comparing the number of cards read with the number of buffers accepted for transmission we can ensure that the card reader pauses before buffer space runs out.

Line Printer is initially suspended waiting for buffers containing data to be printed, to be queued. Executive will reactivate the task as soon as its input queue is non-empty. Similar to the line interface transmitter task, the line printer task queues messages for the line interface receiver task to indicate that buffers have been printed to prevent buffer space becoming exhausted. This method of flow control using returned messages can be eliminated if the executive's queueing mechanism keeps a count of the number of entities in each queue, which can then be obtained by tasks hoping to place entries in that queue. This would increase the complexity of the executive but also increase the efficiency of the system.

Console Input — A buffer is passed to the executive console keyboard handler awaiting any operator message to be typed, and the task is suspended. As soon as a complete message has been assembled the executive activates the task which then queues the message for the line interface transmitter and passes a fresh buffer to executive to use for subsequent typed input. The task is then resuspended.

Console Output is suspended awaiting data for printing on the console to be placed in its queue. As soon as the queue contains an entry, executive wakes it and it passes the message to the executive console printer handler. The task is then suspended until the message has been printed; it is then desuspended enabling it to either dequeue the next message, or if none exists, to suspend awaiting a non empty queue. Neither the console input nor console output tasks need to use the flow control mechanisms described for the line printer and card reader tasks, as the volume of data involved with these devices is generally rather small.

This simplified description of the functioning of basic RJE computer software serves to emphasise the near impossibility of performing even this simple function without the use of an executive to allow the logical functions to be split up and permit well-defined communication between them. There are a great number of these simple executives available, especially for the PDP11; probably there are as many implementations as there are organisations supplying small free-standing remote job entry computers or terminal control processors.

4.3.2 A Commercial Real Time Operating System

In almost all computer data links, at least one end of the link will be a host system; that is, one on which actual work is performed. The other end of the link may be another host, or a remote terminal concentrator or job submission station. The operating systems of almost all computers can be considered as a real time program interacting directly with the computer's hardware. In some systems the only way to write real time tasks, for example, to control communications lines, maybe to add new sections to the operating system. Others are structured so that tasks may be written to run on top of the operating system, but are still able to access the registers of the peripheral devices and to have priority over other users' tasks so that they can respond quickly to external events. An operating system of this type is produced by Digital Equipment Corporation to run on PDP11 systems called RSX-11M. A version is also produced to run small dedicated systems without any backing store devices called RSX-11S, which would be a suitable executive to use for a terminal control processor or the remote job entry system described previously. In this section we describe the facilities available to tasks running under RSX-11M. Most of the 'executive directives' (as they are termed) are available in several forms depending on where and how the parameters to be stored are passed; many also have a large number of parameters which we do not need in describing the overall facilities provided. Readers are therefore referred to the appropriate technical guide to find exact details of the variations and parameters of the functions described here, the function names given will be correct, however.

4.3.3 Some Facilities of RSX-11M

All input/output in RSX-11M is asynchronous; a task queues a buffer either to receive data from some external peripheral, or containing data to be sent. Once the buffer has been queued by a call to the QIO (Queue Input/Output) function processing may continue. Often tasks do not wish to make use of this facility; if they issue a 'read' they wish to wait until the read has been performed, or if a 'write' is issued they must await its completion before writing new data to the buffer they use. The Event Flag system is used to synchronise such activities. There are a large number of these event flags available, each with a numeric value. The lower numbered flags are local to the task, a set exists for each task in the system. The higher numbered ones are global and common to all tasks, hence they can be used to synchronise activities in separate tasks. The state of each flag can be either set or unset. If in the QIO function call an event flag parameter is specified, that flag is cleared when the function is executed and is not set until the input or output has been completed. The function WTSE (Wait for Single Event flag) will cause execution of a task to be suspended until the event flag given as a parameter has been set. In order to overlap processing with input/output as much as possible the task should execute as much as possible before issuing the WTSE directive, that is, it should be placed just before the first reference to the buffer which was queued for the peripheral operation.

The alternative method of notification of some external event, such as the completion of an input or output request is by means of the 'Asynchronous

System Trap' or AST. This is analagous to an interrupt in the hardware of the computer, but implemented in software. When an AST parameter is used in a directive, it is given as the starting address of a routine to be executed. The routine is similar to a subroutine except that instead of being called at some point in the executing code, it is called at some point in time when some external event has occurred. The AST routine runs at a high priority relative to ordinary tasks, so it should be kept reasonably short. An AST routine is terminated by the ASTX (Asynchronous System Trap Exit) directive, equivalent to a return from a subroutine. As soon as the event which the AST will signify occurs, execution of the task is suspended at whatever point it is at and execution of the AST routine starts. If the routine uses any registers these must be saved before they are altered, otherwise the interrupted task will almost certainly fail when it is resumed. ASTs will still be executed in response to external events even if the task is suspended, for example, waiting for an event flag to be set.

If parts of a task need to be executed at a given interval of time, for example, to send null data messages down an otherwise idle data link, the MRKT (Mark Time) directive can be used. This will either set a specified event flag or enter an AST routine after some time interval, which may be measured in clock ticks (50 or 60 per second), seconds, minutes or hours. The larger time intervals are often useful for producing periodic error reports or similar functions. Where two tasks co-operate, and synchronisation of their actions by global event flags does not provide a sufficient mechanism, data can be sent from one task to another. To send a 13 word packet of data the sending task issues an SDAT (Send Data) directive specifying the name of the task to which the data is to be sent, and the address of the data block to be sent. This block of data is queued by executive until the receiving task issues an RCVD (Receive Data) directive. When the RCVD directive is executed, the data block queued (if one is present) is placed in a specified buffer together with the name of the task that queued it. If the receiving task wishes to be informed when data has been queued for it, it may either wait for a global event flag to be set by the sending task or issue an SRDA (Specify Receive Data AST) directive. This will cause execution of the specified AST whenever data is present in the receive data queue for the task.

If required, tasks can respond directly to interrupts and access the status and data registers of devices directly, rather than using the QIO directive to send data to the executive's device driver. This connection to a physical device is achieved by using the CINT (Connect to Interrupt Vector) directive. This function takes as parameters the vector address being connected to and the address of an interrupt service routine included in the task. As access to memory addresses for the device's status registers will use addresses not normally available to user tasks, it must be given special privileges. By so doing these tasks become dangerous and are liable to crash the system if they malfunction. Almost all communications programs can be written to make use of the safer QIO mechanism. When a QIO directive call is issued it specifies a logical unit number on which the action is to be performed. The logical unit number is associated with a physical device either at run-time, or when the task is generated. Each device or set of similar devices has a device driver to deal with its particular requirements.

These device drivers dequeue data packets queued by QIO directives in users' tasks and perform the necessary actions, initiating either a transmission or preparing for reception. Interrupts are dealt with by the device driver – the issuing task is only informed when the operation has been completed, either by setting an event flag or an AST routine being initiated. The use of logical unit of physical device assignation allows ease of altering a program to run on several different systems. The program would not need to be altered to run with a variety of either character interrupt or direct memory access communications devices as the device drivers will all present the same interface to the program.

4.4 COMMUNICATIONS WITH UNHELPFUL SYSTEMS

4.4.1 Using Existing Communications Software

Frequently the operating systems on main-frame computers do not provide the facilities of RSX-11M, which allow user written tasks to communicate easily with communications devices. If this is the case one can only hope to write communications software by incorporating it into the operating system itself. This may be undesirable or impossible as it may result in the producers of the system being unwilling to maintain it, and often no source code for the system is provided making is impossible to modify or extend. In these cases one must make do with whatever product the manufacturer of the system has provided for use with the communications interface.

Prior to the definition of X.25 most major computer manufacturers had evolved their own protocols for connecting remote job entry terminals and remote terminal concentrators etc. The protocols are not general purpose but are particularly oriented toward driving remote card readers, line printers and other peripherals, examples of these are ICL's 7020 and CDC's 200UT. These protocols allowed the remote submission of jobs on cards or paper tape, the return of output from the main-frame to either tape punch or line printer, and interrogation of the state of the system from a console terminal. We shall examine how such a protocol can be used in a networking environment.

4.4.2 Using ICL7020 in Networks

It may seem inappropriate to refer to obsolete protocols in this time of protocol standardisation, but it can be justified on the grounds that there are many machines likely to remain in use for a considerable time which are not capable of using the CCITT-defined protocols. We shall not here discuss in detail the working of the ICL7020 protocol but instead look at the facilities it provides in the context of the George 3 operating system on a 1900 series ICL machine. The name derives from a hardware device originally used at the remote site to drive the peripherals. The ICL 7020 device is not now used but the protocol it used is widely emulated on small computers both to provide remote job entry, as it was intended for, and to interconnect other large machines. A user task in the George 3 system cannot communicate with the communications device directly and the code within the system is complex and not simple to modify so we shall assume that the software is used unaltered. This will provide input from either a card reader or tape reader into the input job queue for subsequent execution, or send it directly to a named 'file' in filestore. The exact destination of an input job depends on the contents of its first record which must be either a "JOB" command detailing that the subsequent records should be interpreted as job control language, or an "INPUT" record specifying where the following records should be stored in the filestore of the machine. Both "JOB" and "INPUT" are terminated either by a specified string of four characters or by the default of "****". If a card reader is being emulated then each record may not be greater than 80 characters in length. For a paper tape reader the maximum length may be several thousand characters, terminated by a line-feed. The paper tape reader is probably the most useful to emulate. If we only want to provide for job submission or file transfer of simple text files then the system can be used directly. File transfer to the ICL main frame being achieved by preceding the file to be sent with an appropriately generated "INPUT" command and adding a terminator to the end. This simple mechanism does not provide any feedback to the system emulating the remote job entry station other than a console message if the command received is faulty in some way. In order to get a positive reply indicating a successful transfer, or an explicit reason for a failure, we need to arrange a program at the destination which will accept incoming files and monitor the transfer to the appropriate filestore catalogue. This can be achieved by always sending the files to a known place in the filestore having planted information on how the file is to be stored at the head of the file itself. A program is arranged which will periodically read this file if it exists; perform the transfer and return to the source of the file, a file containing confirmation of the success, or otherwise, of the transfer. The file may not exist if no transfer has been invoked since the transfer program was last run.

Obtaining either files or job output from a host to a remote job entry station emulator can prove difficult. The two devices which may normally be simulated are the line printer and tape punch. The latter is preferable as files destined for the line printer will frequently have form feed and other formatting characters inserted by the operating system. The tape punch will normally receive only the characters in the source file, but with some null characters for run-off and some header to make the tape identifiable to the human operator. It may also contain some run-off at the end. In order to eliminate these superfluous characters we can place a string of characters which we do not expect in the data at the start and end of the file to be sent. When data is being received by the tape punch emulator, we throw away the data until the start file string is found and copy the file until the end file string is encountered. To determine the destination of the file we may place the name of the file into which the incoming data is to be placed after the start of file string.

The messages destined for an operator's console of the RJE are probably best sent to the console of the machine running the emulator, and some way should be arranged so that messages can be sent from a console input emulator to the mainframe to make status enquiries. The messages destined for printing may also be scanned for those which can be dealt with automatically so that the correct action may be performed and possibly some reply given with no operator intervention being necessary.

4.4.3 Providing Data Transparency on Non-transparent Links

Some systems provide less specialised communications facilities than the ICL7020 protocol which allow data to be sent to and from a program running within the main frame, subject to certain constraints. Typically the protocol may reserve the characters in the ASCII character set whose values are less than octal 30 for internal use, and the hardware may use the eighth bit for parity so that the maximum value which can be sent is octal 177. If we wished to send the full range of values 0–377 octal (for example to send FTP records) we must expand all the characters which fall outside the permitted range into two characters, so that they are recognisably a split pair and can be reconstructed, and so that they both have permissible values. A possible scheme is described below.

We shall term the bits in an 8 bit character from most to least significant by the letters ABCDEFGH. Any character whose ASCII value is greater than or equal to octal 40, or less than or equal to octal 177 is sent unchanged. Characters with values outside these limits are sent as two successive characters in the following way:

p0011FGH   and   p00ABCDE   (where p refers to the parity bit)

When receiving, a split pair can be detected by checking incoming characters for a value of less than octal 40. If a split pair is detected, the top five bits of the first character must be cleared, by performing a logical 'and' with octal 7, the next character obtained and shifted three bits to the left, that is, multiplied by eight. This second character is logically 'or'd' with the first character to yield a full 8 bit value. This technique may be adapted for use with other systems which impose similar contraints.

If a communications program is to be implemented on a system for which there is insufficient documentation to be confident that the implemention has been correctly designed, the best approach is to look at the code produced by someone else for the same machine. This will probably exist buried in the existing operating system of the machine if the source code is available, for some manufacturer's specific protocol. Alternatively, it may be possible to find someone who has implemented something similar by looking through publications produced by other organisations with the same machine. Unless the organisation is a software house who must sell their goods to survive, the chances are high that the source code may be obtained for a nominal fee to cover handling, or perhaps in exchange for some code needed at their organisation produced by yours.

CHAPTER 5

Protocols

5.1 WHY WE NEED PROTOCOLS

A protocol is a set of rules defining the format in which data is to be sent, and the timings when sending between two communicating tasks. When communication is taking place between a computer and a human the protocol can be very simple as the human does not type very fast and has good error detecting facilities – the brain. When typing at the keyboard of a terminal connected to a computer operating in full duplex mode, each character is sent to the computer immediately the key has been pressed. As soon as the computer receives the character it echoes it back to the display on the terminal. As the character on the display is an echo of what the computer received and not just produced within the terminal any errors in the transmission in either direction are apparent as the wrong character appears on the display. This method of error detection is inefficient as it involves 100% feedback of the information sent. A protocol for communication between computers will normally define some parity check and block check mechanism combined with automatic repeat request to retransmit messages containing errors. Where there are several peripherals or logical destinations at each end of a link we need some way of specifying within the transmission the desired destination for each message. When a link is idle we need to agree on some null message to be exchanged to ensure that the data link is still functioning.

   In this chapter we shall first describe a simple protocol used for remote job entry computers with a very limited range of bulk transfer peripherals. A protocol based on similar concepts but with greater sophistication is then described which can deal with a variable mix of devices attached to a cluster. It provides functions to facilitate efficient access for interactive terminals as well as bulk devices. Finally we describe an X.25 network which enables virtual connections to be made over a network of switching computers which can then be used to carry higher level protocols for remote job entry, terminal access, file transfer etc.

5.2 THE ICL 7020 PROTOCOL

5.2.1 Outline of the facilities provided

The 7020 protocol was used to connect an ICL remote job entry terminal type
7020 to a main-frame. The protocol allows for a console terminal, line printer,
tape punch, card reader and tape reader. Each terminal is allocated an address,
and the peripherals a sub-address. This allows several 7020 RJE terminals to be
connected by a multidrop data link to a single main-frame. All the characters
sent on the link are protected by an odd parity bit. The protocol uses several of
the ASCII control characters so only text may be transmitted as data; it is not
a transparent link. The link is half duplex with each end using it alternately. The
main-frame end of the link is termed the *control* terminal and the RJE terminal
the *tributary* terminal. The tributary must reply rapidly to the demands of the
control or it will be assumed that the tributary has crashed. When the control
terminal believes the tributary is down it will poll it at 1/16th the normal idling
rate, for example, once in 64 seconds rather than every 4 seconds. The specification of the protocol which follows is not definitive, the reader is referred to
the ICL publication *TP4328(4.73) Data Communication and Interrogation*, for
the official definition.

We will first define some of the special characters used in the 7020 protocol
and then describe the protocol making reference to these characters.

Table 5.1 – Terminal Address Bit
Assignments.

Terminal	Bit			
	7	6	5	4
1	0	1	0	0
2	0	1	0	1
3	0	1	1	0
4	0	1	1	1
5	1	0	0	0
6	1	0	0	1
7	1	0	1	0
8	1	0	1	1
9	1	1	0	0
10	1	1	0	1
11	1	1	1	0
12	1	1	1	1
Null	0	0	0	0

Bits 1 to 3 are used to provide three peripheral sub-address bits according to Table
5.2.

5.2.2 The 7020 Address Characters

The bits in a character are numbered from 1 to 8 from the least to most significant bits. Bit 8 is always used to make the parity of the character odd. Bits 4 to 7 are used to provide four terminal addressing bits according to Table 5.1.

Table 5.2 — Peripheral Sub-address Bit Assignments.

Device	Bit		
	3	2	1
Terminal	0	0	0
Peripheral 1	0	0	1
Peripheral 2	0	1	0
Peripheral 3	0	1	1
Peripheral 4	1	0	0
Peripheral 5	1	0	1
Peripheral 6	1	1	0
Not used	1	1	1

Peripherals 1, 3, and 5 are always source addresses, that is, they produce data to be sent.
Peripherals 2, 4, and 6 are always acceptor addresses, that is, they receive data sent to them.

The normal assignments of peripherals to a sub-address is as follows:

1 = Paper Tape Reader   4 = Line Printer
2 = Paper Tape Punch   5 = Console Key Board
3 = Card Reader   6 = Console Printer

These assignments are not fixed and should be checked at each site before use.

The terminal and peripheral addresses are combined to form the address of a particular peripheral on a specified terminal, for example, the console printer on terminal 5 would be addressed by an address character with the bit pattern 01000110.

5.2.3 7020 Status Characters

There are two status characters used in the 7020 protocol; *terminal* and *acceptor* status characters. The former is used to provide information from a tributary terminal to the control terminal concerning the status of all its peripherals, the latter to provide more specific details of a particular peripherals' status.

In a terminal status character, bits 1 to 6 are set on if the respective peripheral is operable, or off if it is not. The normal status for an acceptor peripheral such as a line printer is operable, unless it has been switched off-line for some reason. Source peripherals are normally inoperable unless there is data to be sent, if for example the card reader contains cards and has been switched on-line. Bit 7 is always set.

The bit assignment for an acceptor status character are as follows:

Bit	Meaning
1	Set = Acceptor operable
2	Unset = Warning
3	Unset = Attention
4	Unset = Acceptor error
5	Unset = Busy
6	Set = Odd block number, Unset = Even block number
7	Always set

The acceptor status character is used in replying to each data block sent to an acceptor during the data transmission phase, hence bit 6 will alternate between set and unset as each block is sent. This is to ensure that the response refers to the correct data block even if a whole message is lost. The meanings of bits 2–5 are device dependent and the reader is referred to the ICL definition for full details.

5.2.4 Other 7020 Terminology

The following ASCII control characters are used within 7020 – STX, ETX, ETB, EOT, ENQ, ACK, NAK. 'Sync' is used to refer to the two or more ASCII 'SYN' characters preceding each message to enable the receiver to achieve character synchronisation. Data transmission blocks are protected by a block check character (BCC) which is calculated by adding without carry ('exclusive-or' ing) the characters in the message with the exception of the leading STX. This character is appended to the end of the message.

Selecting occurs when the control terminal requests an acceptor peripheral on a tributary terminal to accept data. *Polling* refers to the control terminal inviting a source peripheral on a tributary terminal to send data. The *master* terminal is the terminal currently sending users data; the *slave* is the receiver of the data. Note that control or tributary terminal can be a master or a slave but during the data transmission phase only one terminal will be master and one slave.

5.2.5 Operation of 7020 Protocol

When the control terminal has no data to send to the tributary it will make a status enquiry every few seconds. This acts as a null message to ensure that the data link is still functioning and also checks the status of the peripherals on the tributary.

In this description diagrams representing the characters sent on the data link will be separated by the '/' symbol, which is not actually sent. The characters named in upper case are either ASCII control characters or the special 7020 protocol characters defined earlier. Where 'data' in lower case appears, this refers to a string of characters representing up to 80 characters of users' data either from or to a peripheral on a tributary terminal. All messages are preceded by two or more SYN characters.

The status enquiry frame and the tributary's response are:

Control – Tributary
/EOT/TERMINAL ADDRESS/ENQ/

Tributary — Control
/TERMINAL ADDRESS/TERMINAL STATUS/ACK/

where TERMINAL ADDRESS is as defined in 5.2.2, and TERMINAL STATUS as in 5.2.3. EOT, ENQ, and ACK are ASCII control characters.

If the frame /EOT/NULL ADDRESS/ENQ is sent from the master to the tributary the system should be completely reset; no reply is generated.

If the control terminal has determined that an acceptor peripheral is operable on the tributary and it has data to send it will select the acceptor device. This is done by the selection sequence as follows:

Control – Tributary
/EOT/ ACCEPTOR ADDRESS/ENQ/

Tributary — Control
/ACCEPTOR ADDRESS/ACCEPTOR STATUS/ACK/

where ACCEPTOR ADDRESS is defined as in 5.2.2 and ACCEPTOR STATUS as in 5.2.3. The control terminal now assumes master status and the tributary slave status. Immediately the acceptor status is returned from the tributary the control terminal sends data messages which are described later. The data messages pass the users' data to the acceptor peripheral which has been selected. In order to select a different peripheral, or when the data has ended, the control terminal will cease sending data messages and revert to status enquiry frames as described above.

If the control terminal recognises from its status enquiries that a source peripheral on the tributary has data to be sent, for example, a console message has been typed or the tape reader operated, it will poll the device to accept the data. The sequence to poll a source peripheral is sent:

Control — Tributary   /EOT/SOURCE ADDRESS/ENQ/

The tributary responds with data messages. The tributary is now the master and the control terminal slave. To indicate to the control terminal that the tributary is relinquishing its master status when the data has all been sent it issues the frame:

Tributary — Control   /EOT/

after which the master reverts to status enquiries or further polls or selections.

When a device has been polled or selected data is sent from the master to the slave terminal. If a select has been performed on an acceptor peripheral on the tributary then *it* is the slave and the control is master, the opposite applying if a source peripheral has been polled.

Each data message is terminated by either the ASCII ETX or ETB character followed by the block check character (BCC) described in 2.5. The generation of BCC will be described in the next section. The character ETB is used to terminate data blocks within a message or what can be considered as a file of data; ETX is used to terminate that message or file. Thus a short command from the console input device would consist of a single data message terminated by ETX, whereas each of a card deck would be separated by ETB with ETX being sent after the last card.

Thus data message frames are formatted:

        Master – Slave   /STX/data/ETB/BCC/
or   /STX/data/ETX/BCC/

where 'data' is up to 80 characters of users data.

The slave may reply to the master in one of two ways: if the data received had correct parity settings on all characters, and the BCC generated at the slave agreed with that sent by the master, a positive response is sent; otherwise, a negative response is returned. If a positive response is sent back the next data message will be sent by the master, otherwise the last data message will repeated.

The positive response is:

        Slave – Master   /ACCEPTOR STATUS/ACK/

and the negative:

        Slave – Master   /ACCEPTOR STATUS/NAK/

where NAK is an ASCII control character.

The ACCEPTOR STATUS character is returned even if the control terminal is the slave, because in effect the main-frame is acting as an acceptor peripheral receiving data from a source on the tributary.

If at any stage the tributary does not receive a data block of any kind from the control when one is expected it must remain quiescent. After a long period, say 60 seconds, it may produce an audible or visual warning to indicate that the link has ceased to function; it may not send any data to the control except in reply to data packets. If the control does not receive a reply to a data frame within 2 seconds it will send recovery enquiry packets with the format:

        Control – Slave   /ENQ/

It will send this recovery enquiry every 0.5 to 2 seconds for up to 20 seconds. If the slave detects a recovery enquiry message it either repeats its previous response or sends a negative response if it had been polled. If the control receives no reply to its recovery enquiry than it will produce warnings to indicate the failure and revert to slow status enquiries at one sixteenth the normal rate for status enquiries on an otherwise idle link.

Typical message sequences for polling and selecting are given below, where '3' represents terminal address 3, '33' terminal 3 source peripheral 3, and '34' terminal 3 acceptor peripheral 4.

Polling:

Control	Tributary '3'
/EOT/'3'/ENQ/	
	/'3'/TERMINAL STATUS/ACK/
/EOT/'33'/ENQ/	
	/STX/data/ETB/BCC/
/STATUS/ACK/	
	/STX/data/ETX/BCC/
/STATUS/ACK/	
	/EOT/
/EOT/'3'/ENQ/	

Selecting:

Control	Tributary '3'
/EOT/'3'/ENQ/	
	/'3'/TERMINAL STATUS/ACK/
/EOT/'34'/ENQ/	
	/'34'/ACCEPTOR STATUS/ACK/
/STX/data/ETB/BCC/	
	/STATUS/ACK/
/STX/data/ETX/BCC/	
	/STATUS/ACK/
/EOT/'3'/ENQ/	

If, when a 'status enquiry' 'poll' or 'select' is received, the terminal address contained in it is not the terminal address expected by the tributary the message should be ignored. In a multidropped configuration several 7020 terminals may be successively addressed by the control terminal, selecting or polling devices on a particular terminal as required, the other terminals must ignore data messages unless a peripheral under their control has been selected.

5.2.6 7020 Implementation In Practice

The 7020 protocol is not critical with regard to timing, and up to two seconds can elapse before recovery enquiry messages are sent. This makes the implementation of emulators for 7020 tributaries simple. There is no need to overlap reading from or writing to a file for input or output with processing the incoming data frames. When implemented on a PDP11 running the real time executive RSX-11M operating system, the main body of code can be executed as an AST routine initiated whenever data is received from the data link. A flow chart for the operation of an AST driver 7020 emulator is given in Fig. 5.1. When the

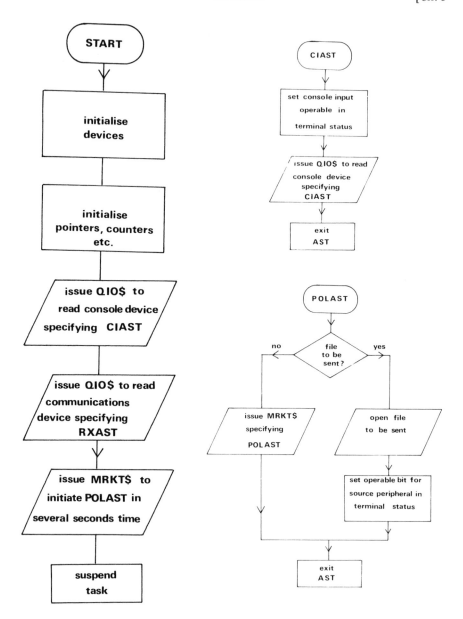

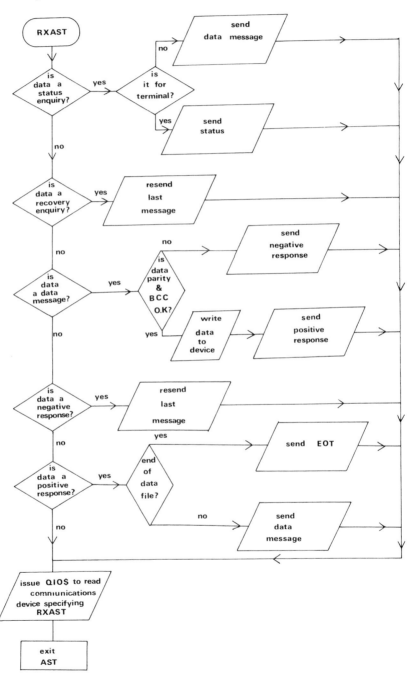

Fig. 5.1 – Flow chart for the operation of an AST driver 7020 emulator.

program is initiated the code initialises the communications device and sets any pointers etc. to their initial values. It then issues QIOs to read data from the data communications device specifying 'RXAST' as the AST routine to be executed when data has been received, and to read data from the console input device specifying 'CIAST' as its AST routine. A timer is also initiated by an MRKT directive which will cause an AST to be executed after a few seconds. This routine, called 'POLAST', checks to see if there is any file to be sent and if there is the source peripheral status bit is set on to indicate it is operable, otherwise a MRKT directive is issued to check again after another time interval. After the initialisation has been performed the task is then suspended so that no resources are used except when an AST occurs.

We shall now give examples of PDP11 assembler code to set and check parity and the block check character added to data messages. Reasonable efficiency is important here as every character transmitted needs to have odd parity and all blocks of considerable size sent are data messages which need the BCC; a considerable overhead could be placed on the machine if an inefficient method is used. Some machines have hardware instructions for adding or checking parity bits, but the PDP11 does not. A possible method of checking parity is to shift the bit pattern representing the character left, one bit at a time, seven times. The sign bit can be tested after each shift with a 'test byte' instruction and a counter incremented each time the sign bit is set. After the seven shifts the bottom bit of the counter can be tested to see whether it is set or clear indicating either odd or even parity. The parity bit could then be set on by a 'bit set' instruction if required. This operation would take about 35 instructions per character which could be a considerable overhead at a reasonable line speed. A faster method is to use a look-up table. This table consists of 128 entries containing the values 0 to 127 but with the appropriate setting of the parity bit. To set parity on any ASCII character we replace the character with the value in the table at the position given by the numeric value of the character. To save readers the tedious task of creating this table it is provided in Table 5.3.

The PDP11 does provide an 'exclusive-or' instruction which can be used to generate a BCC. The code required to add parity to each of a string of characters and generate a BCC at the same time is now given. We assume that a table PARTAB has been set up as shown in Table 5.3, and that R0 contains the start address of the string and R1 its length.

```
CLRB BCCTOT              ; BCC is accumulated in this byte
L: MOVB (R0),R2          ; Get character from string
   BICB #200,R2          ; Ensure parity bit is clear
   MOVB PARTAB(R2),(R0)+ ; Replace by entry with parity, then
                         ; point at next character
   XOR R2, BCCTOT        ; Generate BCC
   SOB R1,L              ; Subtract 1 from R1 and branch to 'L'
                         ; if not zero
```

Table 5.3 – Table to Generate Odd Parity ASCII Characters.

```
PARTAB:    .BYTE  200,001,002,203,004,205,206,007
           .BYTE  010,211,212,013,214,015,016,217
           .BYTE  020,221,222,023,224,025,026,227
           .BYTE  230,031,032,233,034,235,236,037
           .BYTE  040,241,242,043,244,045,046,247
           .BYTE  250,051,052,253,054,255,256,057
           .BYTE  260,061,062,263,064,265,266,067
           .BYTE  070,271,272,073,274,075,076,277
           .BYTE  100,301,302,103,304,105,106,307
           .BYTE  310,111,112,313,114,315,316,117
           .BYTE  320,121,122,323,124,325,326,127
           .BYTE  130,331,332,133,334,135,136,337
           .BYTE  340,141,142,343,144,345,346,147
           .BYTE  150,351,352,153,354,155,156,357
           .BYTE  160,361,362,163,364,165,166,367
           .BYTE  370,171,172,373,174,375,376,177
```

When R1, containing the length of the string falls to zero by the execution of the 'substract one and branch if non zero' instruction, the instruction following SOB R1,L will be executed and the complete string will have odd parity set. A block check character, without parity, is generated in BCCTOT.

Complete PDP11 code is now given to check the parity and BCC of a received 7020 data message. The format of this message is either:

```
        /STX/data/ETB/BCC/
or      /STX/data/ETX/BCC/
```

It should also be remembered that the initial STX character is not included in accumulating the BCC. R0 is assumed to contain the starting address of the string.

```
          CLR BCCTOT
TPAR:     INC R0                    ; Point at next character, ignore
                                    ; first STX
          MOVB (R0),R2             ; Get character from string
          BICB #200,R2            ; Clear whatever parity it had
          CMPB (R0),PARTAB(R2)    ; Compare received character with
                                    ; table entry
          BNE PERR                 ; Parity error if not equal
          XOR R2,BCCTOT            ; Generate BCC
          CMPB R2, #ETX            ; End of string if ETX
          BEQ ETXB
```

```
          CMPB R2,#ETB              ; or ETB
          BNE TPAR                 ; Check next character if not the end
   EXTB:  MOV BCCTOT,R2            ; Got to end of message
          MOVB PARTAB(R2),BCCTOT
                                   ; Add parity to our generated BCC
          INC R0                   ; Point at received BCC
          CMPB BCCTOT,(R0)
          BEQ PAROK                ; Jump to PAROK if parity and BCC
                                   ; are OK
   PERR:                           ; Perform error processing
             ⋮
   PAROK:                          ; Deal with valid message
```

5.3 THE ICL 'XBM' PROTOCOL

5.3.1 Outline of XBM Facilities

The Extended Basic Mode (XBM) protocol is used on both ICL1900 and 2900 range of computers, it is also referred to as CO2. Unlike the 7020 protocol it was never based on a hardware implementation and hence employs considerably more sophistication. The protocol is not dedicated to a fixed configuration of peripherals as 7020 is: interactive terminals as well as bulk input or output devices can be supported. The design also releases the control terminal of the need to poll the devices on the cluster, which if there are many can be a big overhead. The specification is formally defined in ICL document TAS002. The reader is referred to the manufacturers' definition for full details: we shall only describe the system in outline here.

XBM is a two-way alternate protocol; it operates in half-duplex mode with the control terminal sending commands to which the tributary terminal must reply. If no reply is received within the time-out period then error recovery will take place. The protocol does not provide transparency for the text that is transmitted (which may not contain any of the control characters used in the protocol). As before, we will separate fields in a data frame with '/', fields named in upper case represent single control characters, either from the ASCII character set or specific to the protocol. Fields printed in lower case represent multiple character fields.

5.3.2 XBM Address Fields

Control Terminal Address and Control Field — 'cad' is a two-character field used to identify an individual peripheral on a particular terminal, it takes the form:

First Character:

PZZYYYXW

P   = Parity bit for the character, odd parity is always used.

ZZYYY = A 5 bit tributary address with ZZ not allowed to be 00 and excluding ZZYYY = 11111, giving a possible addressing range of 23 tributaries.

X = A single bit sequence count alternating between 0 and 1 to check against loss of complete frames.

W = A single control bit with the following significance: In SELECT command frames which contain data for a peripheral on a tributary, if W = 0 the text is normal data to be transferred to the medium, if W = 1 the text is supervisory information requiring control action by the particular peripheral driver such as altering form lengths on a line-printer. In a POLL command frame W = 0 requests a response containing text if possible, else if W = 1 the peripheral status is being requested.

Tributary Address and Control Field – 'tad' is a two-character frame similar in format to 'cad' except that the W bit is only used to distinguish between normal data and supervisory messages in the text field.

The second character of both 'cad' and 'tad' is used to identify the individual peripheral on a tributary cluster. It provides a maximum of 95 sub-addresses for each tributary: bit 8 is used to provide odd parity, bits 6 and 7 may not take the value 00 and the overall value 1111111 is not permitted.

We shall refer to peripheral sub-addresses by the notation Hex ZY/--, where 'ZY' is any valid combination of the ZZYYY bits specifying the cluster address and '--' the 7 bit value of the sub-address of a peripheral within the cluster.

The following values of addresses have predefined functions:

Hex ZY/20 = Group Control – see 5.3.6
Hex ZY/21 = Reserved
   to ZY/2F
Hex ZY/30 upwards = Available for peripherals

Fig. 5.2 shows a schematic representation of the addressing of XBM peripherals within a cluster.

5.3.3 XBM Control Terminal Frames

General Link-level Reset

/EOT/NUL/NUL/ENQ/

where EOT, NUL and ENQ are ASCII control characters. This frame is actioned by all tributary terminals on an optionally multidropped link to a control terminal and has the effect of clearing any sequence counts and any outstanding requests for retransmission.

Poll

/EOT/cad/ENQ/

where 'cad' is the control address character pair defined in 5.3.2.

A Poll is used to solicit either a new response from the peripheral addressed in 'cad' containing text (Positive Acknowledgement with Texts), a repeat of the previous text response, or a status response. The frame can also acknowledge the last text response depending on the setting of the 'X' bit in 'cad'; this is discussed in 5.3.5. If the W bit of 'cad' is set a status response is required.

Select

/SOH/cad/STX/text/ETX/BCC/

where SOH, STX and ETX are ASCII control characters, BCC is a block check character generated as described in 2.5 but excluding the initial SOH.

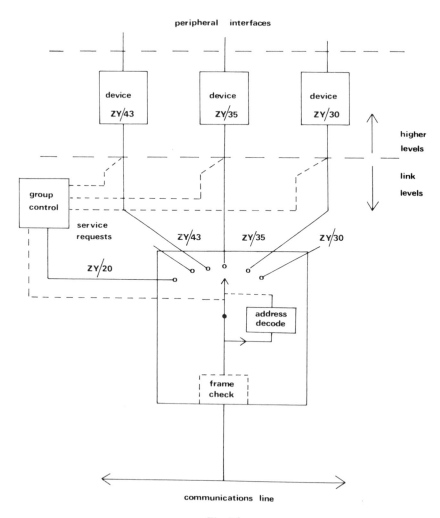

Fig. 5.2.

The Select is used to request a tributary peripheral addressed by 'cad' to accept the text. If the W bit in 'cad' is set the text is supervisory, destined for controlling the driver program for the peripheral, else if the W bit is unset the text is destined for the physical medium controlled by the peripheral driver program. The setting of the sequence count X bit in 'cad' can acknowledge the previous response from the tributary.

5.3.4 XBM Tributary Terminal Frames

Positive Acknowledge with Text

/SOH/tad/STX/text/ETX/BCC/

This frame is used by a tributary to return data in response to a Poll frame from the control terminal. The data is supervisory if the W bit in 'tad' is set, otherwise the data is input from the device.

Positive Acknowledgement Without Text

/STATUS1/STATUS2/ACK/

where STATUS1 is the tributary link level status character defined as follows:

Bit	Meaning if Set
1	Always unset
2	Service Request
3	Always unset
4	Link level has reset
5	High level failure (data lost)
6	Link level sequence error
7	Always set
8	Parity

The STATUS2 character is set in a device-specific manner.

The Positive Acknowledgement without Text is sent in response to a Poll from the Control terminal when no text is available for transmission, or when a status reply is requested. It is also sent after a successful Select when the text is received without error.

Negative Acknowledgement (no text)

/STATUS1/STATUS2/NAK/

where NAK is the ASCII control character. This frame is used to respond to a Select which contained an error in either the parity of a character, the BCC or a sequence count error.

5.3.5 Summary of Tributary Responses

Command	'cad' W bit	Description	Tributary response	
			'X' out of sequence	'X' in correct sequence
Poll	Unset Set	Send Status Send Text	Status ACK[*] response to previous in sequence command	Status ACK New text or Status ACK
Select	Unset Set	Data Supervisory	Status NAK[*] Status NAK[*]	Status ACK[†] Status ACK[†]

[*] With sequence error status.
[†] Assumes text received without errors.

Each peripheral driver on a tributary and each corresponding driver in the control terminal maintains a sequence count. The sequence count occupies only one bit and so alternates between zero and one each time the sequence count is advanced. As a sequence counter exists for each peripheral and commands or responses can be solicited from peripherals in any order by the control terminal, the sequence count for all frames to a tributary may not alternate, but they will for each address within the tributary. Initially, or after a general link level reset all sequence counters will be zero. The command numbered n to a specific tributary acknowledges the receipt of the response to the command numbered $n - 1$. Thus a select command can acknowledge a previous text response to a poll. If the tributary receives a sequence count which does not correspond to that expected it responds with an 'X out of sequence' reply. Error recovery is the responsibility of the control terminal so the tributary must always reply in strict accordance with the received command. The sequence count for each peripheral driver is incremented once for each cycle consisting of a command sent by the control terminal and a reply sent by the tributary.

5.3.6 Group Control

Group control is a special tributary in all clusters with more than one peripheral. Although group control is accessed by the basic link level multiplexing action, it is itself a part of the link level. It enables an XBM cluster to act as a concentrator in that it allows a single poll command addressed to it to solicit data from any of the other peripherals. The response sent looks similar to those produced by directly addressing the device. Group control contains a list of devices from which it can accept service requests. A service request is made whenever a peripheral has data ready to be sent. The list of devices kept by group control is called the 'poll list'. Initially it contains all the devices on the cluster. Select commands may be sent to group control containing supervisory messages to cause it to empty its poll list, or add or remove specific sub-addresses from the list. The devices on the poll list are scanned cyclically so that if several devices raise service requests they will all be serviced with group control choosing the order rather than the control terminal. If a data poll is sent to group control it can either reply with text from a tributary or with a status reply if there is no data to be sent. If a status poll is sent a status reply is sent with the 'service request' bit set in STATUS1. Group control never includes a STATUS2 character in a status reply. Group control will ignore any select commands containing ordinary text as invalid and it will be ignored.

5.3.7 XBM Implementation Notes

XBM is a strictly half-duplex protocol basically similar to 7020 and for use as a remote job entry protocol the implementation would be similar.

If terminals are to be supported the complexity will be considerably increased. The major difficulty is not in providing the protocol handling for terminals but in communicating with terminals which are under the control of the operating system. The problems are not so great if the terminals are dedicated in advance to the task of communicating via XBM. If the terminals are to be able to use the ordinary facilities of the operating system of the machine they are connected to, as well as a remote machine via XBM there needs to be some mechanism for passing messages to and from the XBM program. The simplest mechanism would probably be to have a task which each user would invoke and which would communicate with the XBM program by some inter-process message passing mechanism.

5.4 THE STRATHCLYDE X.25 NETWORK – A CASE STUDY

5.4.1 Overview

Strathclyde University has operated a packet switched network since about 1975, before the CCITT standard protocols were defined. The protocols used were designed locally in conjunction with Glasgow and Edinburgh Universities. The network operated in a triangular topology with nodes at each of the three universities. The nodes were originally comprised of CTL Modular One computers each with about 56K words of main memory and several synchronous line interfaces. At a later date some of the nodes were replaced by PDP11 computers. The protocol used was called NSI (Node Standard Interface) and contained essentially the features to be found in X.25 but in a simpler and less clearly defined manner, such as the creation of virtual circuits and the ability to send

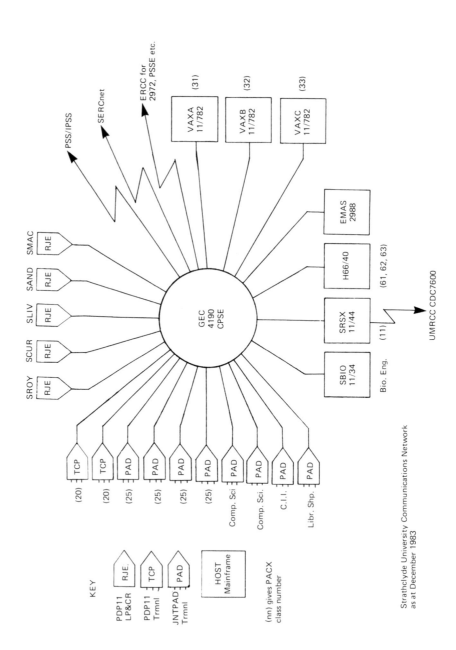

Fig. 5.3

small amounts of data outside the flow control constraints of the system to perform actions requiring immediate response such as a break-in from an interactive terminal. NSI also contained a feature not found in most of todays networks in having a data-gram facility whereby a small amount of data can be sent without having to set up a virtual circuit. This type of feature is useful for the implementation of several applications, for example a network information server which operates by sending requests for a small amount of information to devices on a network to ascertain their status — the number of users currently using a PAD or the status of an RJE station for example.

Figure 5.3 shows the state of the Strathclyde University communications network as at December 1983. The old Modular One node processor has been scrapped and replaced by a commercially available Packet Switched Exchange (PSE) which is produced by GEC Computers Limited to a specification derived from the Joint Network Team — a sub-committee of the Computer Board set up to encourage standardisation of communications facilities in the U.K. academic community. We have in the United Kingdom achieved a very well integrated communications system due to the enforcement of standards by this body. An obvious choice for a communications standard for a community of such a heterogeneous nature as the academic one is a packet switched network standard with international acceptance, X.25 being the only serious contender. Given this basic foundation it was necessary to find high level protocols that could implement the sorts of functions which users require, typically interactive access, remote job submission, file transfer, and electronic mail. The CCITT and ISO are still a considerable way from defining standards at these higher levels so protocols have had to be defined in advance and implemented. This effort has resulted in the definition and widespread implementation of the so called 'Rainbow Books' which define high level protocols for the use of the U.K. academic community. X.25 cannot be used alone to carry data in our community because it does not permit the interconnection of networks in a convenient manner. For political reasons each institution is considered to be a separate entity at the present time and many, such as Strathclyde, run their own networks internally. This gives rise to the problem of address domains. The owner of any network is allowed to choose the network addresses within that network, where two networks are connected there is potentially a problem that both networks may use the same address for different hosts in different parts of their own networks, a mechanism is needed to keep the address ranges of different networks which are interconnected separate. This function is performed by a device called a gateway. This is a host on both of the networks to which it is connected. For example a gateway is to be found as one of the internal processes in the GEC PSE at Strathclyde between the PSE and the PSS and also the SERC connections. These are both networks operated by bodies outside the University, the former being the national packet switched network operated by British Telecom and the latter being operated by the Science and Engineering Research Council, both have their own addressing schemes which cannot be controlled by Strathclyde nor do they cooperate with each other, potentially then we could have three-way clashes of address at Strathclyde. For an interactive terminal using the CCITT standard protocols X.3, X.28 and X.29 above X.25 the gateway can hold a conversation with the user to decide where to send the call. Thus a user in Strathclyde University can call from one of the PADs PSS, this gets him to the gateway in the GEC PSE which protects the PSS line. The gateway software then asks the user for the address that the user wants to connect to on the PSS network and then makes a call to that address on behalf of that user to the address, it then plays no further part in the communication being quite transparent to the user. In the reverse situation if a user on a PAD connected in some way to PSS calls our address he arrives on the other side of this gateway and is required to give the address to which he wants to make a connection within the Strathclyde domain. This is reasonably satisfactory for interactive users, but rather tedious if several gateways have to be traversed, it is not satisfactory for computer to computer connections though. It would be possible to automate the replies given to the prompts given by each of the gateways if the prompts given by the various gateways were in some way standardised – but they are not, and nor is it either likely or desirable that they should be since they often approach the needs of different groups of users with different levels of sophistication and expectations. The problem is solved by the addition of a protocol layer above the X.25 packet level. That it is above the X.25 level gives it the advantage that it can be used in environments where it is not considered to be appropriate to run a packet switched network and also gives an easy path to future systems of communications technology. Many Universities which are arranged around a compact site can use one of the high speed local area network technologies such as the Cambridge Ring or Ethernet with a communications server attached to it to give access to the wider community. The Transport Service in widespread use in the United Kingdom is the Yellow Book Transport Service (YBTS). This provides a process to process virtual circuit with features similar to the X.25 network upon which it often runs, for example an Expedited facility to rush small quantities of data disregarding flow control, Reset to clear a connection down to a known state etc. The most important feature is the ability to address across many networks by the use of Transport Service gateways in packet switches making use of the hierarchic addressing allowed by YBTS. An X.25 address consists of a basic 12 digits with an optional 2 digit sub-address. YBTS allows addresses in principle of any length, although typically they are restricted in practice to 255 characters. The addressing system is easiest to explain by example. The address the PDP 11/44 on the network at Strathclyde University as shown on Fig. 5.3 is 71000016, the address of the University on the PSS network is 234241260106. If a process on a computer connected to PSS outside the University wants to connect to the File Transfer Process on the PDP 11/44 which is associated with the title FTP inside the PDP 11/44 computer the address that will be used is:

234241260106.71000016.FTP

This is passed as a text string from the process in the remote computer to its Transport Service which strips the first part of the address up to the first delimiter and uses that to make an X.25 call on behalf of the process, with the call request X.25 packet that is sent out the remainder of the complete address is also sent, in this case:

71000016.FTP

When the call request arrives at the GEC PSE containing this data the GEC gate way software makes a call within the PSE to the address given by the first part of the address that it sees up to the delimiter in exactly the same way as before. Thus when the call request arrives at the PDP 11/44 the data with it consists of:

FTP

The Transport Service module then passes the call request with this data to the process which has been associated with that name.

A similar example in the opposite direction would be the case of the File Transfer Process in the PDP 11/44 calling the corresponding process in the DEC 10 at York University. The address is longer in this case because York University also has a packet switched network so we have to supply information on how to get from the PDP 11/44 to the PSS line on the PSE, the address of York on PSS, the address of the particular DEC 10 in York's network and the process to be used on the DEC 10 when we get there. The actual address to be used would be:

71000006.234290468168.YORKS.FTP

Where 71000006 is the address of the PSS gateway on the Strathclyde PSE, 234290468168 is the address on PSS of York University, YORKS identifies the KS10 processor on the York network and FTP the process to be invoked.

5.4.2 The Protocols Used
The computer network shown in Fig. 5.3 is based upon the use of X.25 and some higher level protocols. We shall here given an outline description of the protocols used going up from the physical transmission methods in use, up through the layers defined by X.25 to the high level protocols used to provide user level functions.

The Physical Level:
In accordance with the specification X.21 bis, V.24 is used to connect most of the host computers, PADs and remote Job Entry stations to the CPSE, at speeds of either 9.6Kbps or 19.2Kbps. The Digital Equipment VAX 11/782 computers

are connected at 48Kbps using the V.35 protocol. The V.35 protocol is for use at speeds greater than 20Kbps, it uses changes in current levels rather than voltage levels and is more immune to noise.

The Link Level:
The HDLC (High-level Data Link Control) procedure called LAP-B is in use to provide error correction and detection and also low level flow control between the network hosts and the CPSE. This protocol is the standard required by British Telecom for use on the national Packet Switch Stream (PSS) service. The LAP-B procedures provide a transparent bidirectional error free virtual channel between two computers. The transparency is provided by 'Bit Stuffing', whenever the hardware of the transmitter in the communications interface detects that five contiguous binary one bits have been sent a binary zero is inserted into the data stream. Whenever the receiver detects five one bits it automatically removes the next (zero) bit from the incoming data stream. The only place where six contiguous one bits are permitted is in the hardware generated and detected 'Flag' byte which delimits a LAP-B frame, this consists of a zero followed by six ones and another zero bit. The interface will have special control bits in its control register to initiate the transmission of Flag bytes or to report their reception. Each frame is protected against corruption in transmission by a two byte Cyclic Redundancy Check which provides a better level of error detection than a simple block check character. The theory of operation of Cyclic Redundancy Checks (CRCs) is described in many papers, for example Kirstein & Higginson (1973). The generation of these CRCs is quite complex in software and is generally performed and checked by hardware in the transmitter and receiver. A complete LAP-B frame is as follows: /Flag/Address/Control/CRC/CRC/Flag/, where each entry between solidus is one byte, or where there is user level information to be carried:

/Flag/Address/Control/Data. . . . . ./CRC/CRC/Flag/,

the Data field can be many bytes long typically 128 or up to 1024. The Address byte is used to indicate which end of the link sent a command in order to distinguish between commands and responses. The values used are termed 'A' and 'B' and take the binary patterns 00000011 and 00000001 respectively. The Control byte indicates the function of the frame, the most important are Information (I), Receiver Ready (RR), Receiver Not Ready (RNR), Reject (REJ), Unnumbered Acknowledge (UA), Set Asynchronous Balanced Mode (SABM), and Disconnect (DISC). The binary representations of these commands can be found in the British Telecom PSS Technical Users Guide – (1983). The operation of the LAP-B protocol will be described textually, for a rigorous description see 'X.25 Explained' by R. J. Deasington (1984). Information frames are used to carry X.25 packets of data for users, the control byte contains two three bit counters termed N(R) and N(S). The N(S) counter contains a value between 0 and 7 representing the sequence number of the information frame, each I-frame sent has a send sequence count N(S) one greater than the previous. The buffer in the transmitter cannot throw away its copy of each I-frame until it has received an acknowledgement for it. This acknowledgement comes in the Receive Sequence count N(R) which is contained in received frames of RR, RNR, I, and REJ. This value is sent by the receiver of I-frames to acknowledge correct receipt of all frames with a sequence number up to N(R) minus one. Any frame received with an invalid FCS check is totally ignored. All frames are transmitted with a timer such that if a response to them is not received within this period they are retransmitted. If an I-frame is received with a sequence number not exactly one greater than the previous a REJ frame is sent with an N(R) value equal to the next expected sequence number, the transmitter must then resend all I-frames from that point onwards. A limit is agreed between the two ends of the link as to how many frames may be sent ahead of the received sequence count, this is called the Window. The I-frame also contains an N(R) field so it can acknowledge I-frames sent in the opposite direction. If the receiver is not able to receive further data in I-frames it can send a Receiver Not Ready, this would typically be done if the receiver software has run out of buffer space, to indicate that the receiver is ready to receive further data a Receiver Ready is sent, these frame types are also sent in response to received I-frames if there is no data to carry in the opposite direction which can carry the revised N(R) count. All the different frame types contain a one bit field termed the Poll/Final bit, if this is set then the receiver must reply immediately rather than wait for some data to arrive to send an acknowledgement and must also set the bit on in the replying frame. This bit is set on in frames which are retransmitted due to the time-out interval allowed for reply having expired. When the link is in the down state the DCE (network) end will send DISC frames at an interval equal to the time-out period. When the DTE (network host) becomes active it will reply to the DISC by sending a UA to acknowledge the control packet followed by the SABM frame to indicate that the link should be restarted. The DCE will reply with a UA to the SABM at which point the link is considered to be up and available for exchange of data in either direction. It should be remembered that this link up state only refers to the 'link level' and that the X.25 packet level will then be restarted. All X.25 packet level information is sent inside I-frames, the purpose of the link level is only to provide an error free virtual channel whose speed can be controlled by the receiver, we shall now describe the packet level.

The Packet level:
An X.25 packet switched network is characterised by the format of information packets that can be entered by a terminal to the network to be delivered, in the same order, to the destination terminal. The route that packets take in their journey from source to destination need not be known to either end and may consist of many links between many packet switched exchanges, as is the case

with PSS the public packet network operated by British Telecom, or through
only one switch as is the case with the Strathclyde University data network. The
full definition of X.25 would take many pages so only a small subset of the
facilities which are available will be described here, for further details the reader
is referred to a more detailed guide to these protocols such as 'X.25 Explained'
by the author. There are two basic types of connection that can exist between
two terminals in an X.25 packet switched network termed Switched Virtual
Call and Permanent Virtual Circuit, generally these are abbreviated SVC and
PVC respectively. An SVC is analogous with a dial-up telephone call where the
connection only exists until one end or the other breaks the connection, whereas
a PVC is analogous with a leased line which is always available. The format of
the first three bytes of a packet is constant and will be described first. It should
be remembered that all X.25 packets are transmitted as LAP-B I-frames as
described earlier. Many SVCs or PVCs can be multiplexed by the X.25 protocol
down one error free vitual channel provided by LAP-B, this multiplexing is
performed by allocating a channel number to each separate X.25 level connection which all packets pertaining to that particular conversation will have in their
header. In British Telecoms PSS network the channel number which is composed
of twelve bits is sub-divided into two parts called the Logical Group Number and
the Logical Channel Number, of four and eight bits respectively. Thus the header
of an X.25 packet has the following layout:

Bit	8	7	6	5	4	3	2	1
Byte 1	Format Ident			/	Logical Group			
	0	0	0	1 /	g	g	g	g
2	Logical Channel							
	e	c	c	c	c	c	c	c
3	Packet Type Identifier							
	t	t	t	t	t	t	t	t

The format identifer of an X.25 packet is always as shown in the uper half of the
first byte. The subsequent bytes have values depending on the Packet Type
Indentifier value. If the packet is an information carrying packet there will be
up to 1024 bytes of user data to be carried, typically though most networks are
operated with a packet size of 128 bytes since this is nearer the typical size that
most users have in interactions with computer systems. A larger packet size is
more efficient for carrying bulk data but means that the buffer size needed by
the transmitter and receiver software needs to be much greater than that which
is normally used and so is therefore wasteful of memory. To establish an SVC

between two networked computers they must send and receive a Call Request/ Incoming Call packet, the format is the same but is termed differently to reflect the two ends of a connection. For an outgoing call the DTE chooses a free channel number by which all future references to this call will be identified. The packet type identifier will take the value Hex 0B followed by a byte containing in two four bit counters the lengths of the calling and called addresses in Binary Coded Decimal (BCD) digits followed by the addresses packed two characters to a byte. The address of a host on an X.25 network consists of between one and twelve decimal digits with an optional two digit subaddress beyond that to identify the destination of the call to the receiving software. The decimal characters are stored in four bits each with a binary value of between 1 and 9. The receiving DTE will receive an Incoming Call packet of identical structure except that the channel number will have been filled in by the network software to reflect a channel which it considers to be free. The channel numbers which may be used are decided when the network link is arranged with the operators of the network and by convention the DTE chooses the highest channel numbers to be used first while the network software chooses the lowest channel numbers which are free in order to minimise clashes when both ends choose the same number at the same time. There are two possible replies to an Incoming Call packet, either Call Accepted which is received by the sender of the Call Request packet as a Call Connected, or Clear Request if the DTE does not wish to accept the call, this is received as a Clear Indication packet. The Call Accept/Call Connected packet has the packet type identifier of Hex 0F and no further information, a Clear Request/Clear Indication packet has a packet type identifier of Hex 13 followed by two bytes which carry a clearing cause and a diagnostic byte which can be provided by the sender of the Clear Request. The Clear Request packet can be sent at any time by either end of an SVC to end the connection or by the network if it detects that the other end of a link has failed or is some intervening link in the connection has failed in which case both ends of the connection will receive a Clear Indication from the network. When a DTE receives a Clear Indication it must reply with a Clear Confirmation to indicate that it consideres the channel to be free, this packet is passed to the initiator of the Clear Request packet and has the packet type identifier value of Hex 17 with no further data. If a Call Request packet is replied to with a Call Accept packet the SVC is considered to be in the data transfer state, data can now be sent in either direction subject to flow control which will now be described. The format of data packets is slightly different to all others and is described now:

Bit	8	7	6	5	4	3	2	1
Byte 1	Q	0	0	1 /	Logical Group			
2	Logical		Channel				Number	
3 /			P(R) /	M /		P(S)		/ 0
	User	Data						

The top bit of the format identifier is used as one of two user definable bits in the packet and is termed the Qualifier bit, this is typically used by higher level protocols which use X.25 to carry messages on their behalf to distinguish between control messages which have significance to the protocol handlers as opposed to actual user data, the meaning is stricly defined between the end users and has no effect on the intervening network. The bit marked 'M' in the third byte is the More bit. This is used to indicate that the data being carried by the packet is part of a larger message which has been split up because it exceeds the maximum packet size. If the More bit is set the packet must be full or the network will signal an error. The P(R) and P(S) fields are used in the same way as the N(R) and N(S) fields in LAP-B which we described earlier, when a call is set up there is an agreed limit of the number of Data packets which can be sent ahead of an acknowledgement being received by the sender of the data. These are three bit counts so the maximum value for the number of outstanding packets is seven. The sequence number for each packet sent is placed in P(S) and the P(R) value indicates that packets with a sequence number up to P(R)-1 have been correctly received. Since the X.25 protocol is operated over an error free virtual channel provided by LAP-B packet sequence numbers should always be in sequence, however to provide for extra protection of the data the sequence number can be tested when received to ensure that it is exactly one greater than the previous one. If a sequence number error is found then a packet level Reject may be sent to request the retransmission of packets from the last in-sequence packet plus one. The first two bytes of a packet level Reject packet follow the usual pattern, the third byte is coded as: rrr11011, where rrr indicates the three bit value of the sequence count that the other end must start to retransmit from. Since packet sequence number errors should be extremely rare this feature is often not implemented in X.25 software. The number of packets which can be outstanding or Window, can be negotiated when the call is set-up using special 'Facilities' fields in the Call Request packet, obviously the larger the window the more buffer space will be required since up to that number of packets of data will have to be kept until acknowledgement is received for them. The acknowledgements for Data packets can be transmitted on Data packets travelling in the opposite direction or sent on packet level Receiver Ready packets if there is no data to be sent in the reverse direction. A packet level Receiver Ready packet has a similar format to that of the packet level Reject where the first two bytes are as normal followed by a third byte with the following coding: rrr00001, where rrr is the three bit value of receive sequence number to be conveyed. If buffer space for a Data packet is temporarily unavailable then a packet level Receiver Not Ready can be sent which operates in the same way as the link level RNR frame in that it causes the other end of a link to cease to send packets of data, the receive sequence count indicates the number of the packet minus one which has been correctly received. The packet level Receiver Not Ready is coded similarly to packet level Reject and Receiver ready as follows:

rrr00101, for the third byte with the rrr again representing a three bit value for the receive sequence count. When a DTE receives a packet level RNR it will cease to send Data packets on that logical channel. It should be remembered that all this packet level flow control applies only to one particular virtual circuit identified by the channel number in the packet and that other channels may continue to transmit and receive even if one channel is blocked by flow control. This facility in X.25 is very useful as it allows the receiver of data to determine the rate at which data is sent by a transmitter simply by only requesting packets of data from the X.25 software when it is ready to receive them. To allow for the case where a DTE wishes to send data to the other end of a connection ignoring flow control constraints an interrupt facility is provided. The Interrupt packet has a packet type identifer of Hex 23 which is followed by one byte of user defined data. The receiver of an Interrupt packet must reply with an Interrupt Confirmation packet before a further one can be sent in that direction. Only one Interrupt packet can be in transit in each direction on a given virtual circuit. The Interrupt Confirmation packet has a packet type identifier of Hex 27 and carries no other data. The interrupt is typically used where a response is required rapidly from a remote system in response to some real time event occurring. A typical case is that of a user of a terminal connected across an X.25 network to an interactive computing facility and listing some text on the terminal, if he wishes to terminate the listings whose output he may have suspended using flow control he will cause an Interrupt packet to be sent to the host computer to indicate to the operating system that the user requires the current task to be broken off and immediate attention given to the user. There are several packet types which are not dealt with here as this is not intended to be a full account such as those which can reset a call thus clearing a hung-up condition and those restart packets used by the X.25 software to indicate to the packet switched exchange that the packet level should be restarted etc. For a full description of the facilities available the reader is referred to a more detailed study of the X.25 protocol.

The Transport Level:
The Transport Service used is the 'Yellow Book Transport Service' defined by Study Group Three of the British Telecom PSS User forum, its title is usually abbreviated to YBTS and Transport Service to TS. TS is not necessarily implemented above an X.25 communications layer, it can be run over Cambridge Rings, Ethernets or any communications medium which allows for the bi-directional transparent transmission of data between two points, the elements of YBTS map very closely on to the facilities provided by an X.25 network however. TS is intended to provide interprocess communications between two tasks which may or may not be in the same physical machine. After a connection has been established between the two processes a transparent bi-directional data stream exists between them, the mechanisms used to transmit this data stream between

the two processes is of no concern to the processes hence it provides a 'future proof' protocol for use by higher level activities such as file transfer etc. Its addressing mechanism overcomes the limitations of strict X.25 addressing by allowing a hierarchical address to be built up and interpreted as the address passes through the network. The complete details of YBTS can be found in the Yellow Book (1980), we shall describe some of its features here but for a formal description the reader is referred to the Yellow Book.

The YBTS provides facilities for Connecting and Disconnecting a call, for Expediting data, for sending Data and also forcing its delivery by the Push operation, and also for Accepting calls and Resetting the state of calls. All of the functions except for Data and Push are sent as X.25 messages with the Modifier bit set on to indicate that this is control data not data intended for the user process. Data to be sent in X.25 Information frames is buffered up so that only full packets are sent so that the More bit is set on, this ensures optimal use of the packet layer and lower layers. This is not convenient if a response is required to some message which does not exactly fill a packet, hence the Push function is provided to force the delivery of all data up to the point in the stream of messages where the Push occurred. A Pushed data message need not be sent as a full packet and the More bit will not be set on. The Connect function takes strings of characters as its arguments, in particular the Called Address and the Calling Address, the former describes to the TS how to set up a call to the destination process and possibly what to do at various gateways in the network route to the destination. The Calling Address will indicate to the receiving process exactly what is calling it, if the File Transfer process is calling the Interactive Terminal Protocol handler the latter would probably reject the call as being erroneous. If the receiving process can handle the incoming Connect it will issue an Accept after which the bi-directional data stream exists between the two processes, in the case of the caller only after the Accept has been received. Once the call is established either end can send Data or Pushes at will, there will be a locally defined mechanism to control the flow of data between the user process and the TS which will depend on the facilities available in the Operating System in the machine and how the TS implementor has arranged things, the transmitter of data does not need to know how fast the receiver of the data is operating as back pressure will cause it to hold off sending further data when the TS and lower levels reach their limit of buffering capability. When the exchange of data between the two processes is finished then either one of them may send a Disconnect which causes the immediate loss of the link, any data in transit being lost, hence the higher level protocol above the TS must be sure that all data has been received before it issues Disconnects. A Disconnect may also be issued in response to an incoming Connect request if the process it is destined for cannot handle the call or it may be issued by the network if it recognises that some part of the network which was in use for the call has just gone out of service. If the high level protocol in use recognises that it has got confused in a connection with another similar protocol handler then it may issue a Reset, this destroys all data in transit, clears down any data which may be being buffered by the network and returns the connection to a state as if it had just been created. The expedited function is used to send small amounts of data outside of flow control constraints, this would be used for example when a terminal user wants to interrupt some process on a mainframe computer that he is connected to over a TS connection using a protocol designed for terminal handling. This facility is mapped onto the X.25 Interrupt function which can only send one byte at a time so by convention messages less than or equal to one byte are sent using this mechanism.

Higher Level Protocols:

The most important high level protocols in use on the Strathclyde University network are those for file transfer, remote terminal access and remote listing of output on line printers connected to small remote job entry computers. File transfer makes use of a protocol defined in this country termed Network Indepenant File Transfer Protocol (NIFTP), almost all academic computing facilities have this available on at least some of their computers so it can be used over PSS and SERC-net as well as within the University network itself. The protocol operates by describing the filestore of each computer in terms of virtual-filestore which is then mapped on to the real filestore of the receiving machine, the code used for the transfer is also the subject of negotiation when the transfer is initiated. The protocol operates over the Yellow Book Transport Service and so can be used in multiple network situations. Terminal access is at present mainly based on the use of a CCITT protocol termed Triple X, which is an abbreviation for X.3, X.28, and X.29 which together describe how character mode terminals should be connected to an X.25 packet switched network. This is accomplished by a device termed a Packet Assembler/Disassembler (PAD) which collects the characters sent by a terminal until some delimiter is reached when it sends off the characters which had been accumulated in a packet to the host computer system. The character or characters which cause this forwarding to take place are under the control of the host computer which can send messages to the PAD to dictate exactly how it should operate. The messages which are sent between the PAD and the host computer system which are involved with setting the various parameters of the PAD are sent as X.25 information packets with the Qualified data bit set on, ordinary data destined for the host is sent as unqualified data. When packets of data are received for a terminal the PAD sends them out one at a time using an asynchronous format. To establish a call to a host the terminal user is required to converse with the PAD to specify to what X.25 address a call should be made to, often this will be in the form of a mnemonic so that the user doesn't need to remember many long strings of digits. Because the Triple X protocols operate directly on an X.25 network only one network hop can be made at a time using Triple X, which in a multiple network environment is a disadvantage. These protocols were defined before the clear advantages of the insertion of a Transport Service had been recognised by the CCITT. In the U.K. we have developed a version of the X.29 protocol (the part which specifies how the data is to be stored in packets) termed TS.29 which operates on top of the YBTS. It does this by using the first byte of each Transport Service Data Unit (TSDU), i.e. each group of Data messages delimited by a Push, instead of using the Qualified data bit in the X.25 packets. This byte is set to zero if the data is unqualified, i.e. ordinary traffic between the terminal and the host system, or 128 if the data following is Qualified and only of interest to the PAD or the terminal handling software in the host. Apart from this alteration there is no other alteration to the standard protocol. This alteration allows users to connect directly to the machine they want in one step instead of having to stop at gateways along the route and tell them the next hop in the route they are trying to traverse, because the protocol is so similar to ordinary X.29 it is very easy to perform a protocol conversion between the two hence it is quite widely supported. For sending listings to remote networked line-printers we initially investigated the use of NIFTP which allows a remote output mode of operation, however we found that the generality of the protocol is such that an implementation could not be fitted in the memory of most of the remote job entry stations available which are 64Kbyte PDP11s. We therefore decided to use TS.29 for this purpose in the reverse of its usual role, in this case the host initiates calls to remote devices on the network rather than conversely. This use of the protocol is quite widespread and was considered to be a 'better' solution to inventing yet another protocol locally.

Electronic Mail is implemented to a definition termed the Grey Book protocol which uses in turn the NIFTP to carry files which contain the mail messages to the required host. This is a very widely used facility and mail is exchanged both between the different machines in the Strathclyde University network and with many hosts in other institutes both in this country and overseas.

Bibliography

Bacon, M. D., and Bull, G. M. (1973), *Data Transmission*, Macdonald.

BBC, ITV, BREMA (1976), *Broadcast Teletext Specification*.

Blanc, R. P. (1974), Assisting users with a Network Access Machine, *Proc. ACM*, p. 74.

British Post Office (1975), *Handbook of Data Communications*, NCC.

British Post Office (1979), *British Post Office PSS Technical Users Guide* (draft).

British Telecom (1983) *PSS Technical Users Guide*.

CCITT (1976), *Recommendation X.25* ('Orange Book'), Tome V111.2.

CCITT (1978), *Recommendations X3, X28 and X29 on Packet Switched Data Transmission Services*, ITU, Geneva.

Data Communications Protocol Unit (1980), *A Network Independent Job Transfer and Manipulation Protocol* ('Red Book'), NPL.

Data Communications Protocol Unit (1981), *A Network Independent File Transfer Protocol* ('Blue Book'), NPL.

Davies, D. W., Barber, D. L. A., Price, W. L., and Solomonides, C. M. (1979), *Computer Networks and their Protocols*, Wiley.

Deasington, R. J. (1984) *X.25 Explained*, Ellis Horwood Ltd.

Hamming, R. W. (1950), Error Detecting and Error Correcting Codes, *Bell Systems Technical Journal*, **XXVI**.

Hwa, H. R. (1975), A Framed ALOHA System, *Proc. PACNET Symposium, Sendai, Japan*, p. 109.

ISO (1976), *Data Communication – High-Level Data Link Control Procedures – Frame Structure*, ISO 3309.

ISO (1978), *Data Communication – High-Level Data Link Control Procedures – Elements of Procedure*, ISO 4335.

ISO (1979), *Reference Model of Open Systems Interconnection*, ISO/TC97/SG16 N227.

Kirstein and Higginson (1973), Cyclic Redundancy Check Computation, *Computer Journal*, p. 19.

McNamara, J. E. (1977), *Technical Aspects of Data Communications*, DEC.

Bibliography

Metcalfe, R. M., and Boggs, D. R. (1976), Ethernet: Distributed Packet Switching for Local Computer Networks, *Comms. of the ACM*, **19**, No. 7.

Study Group 3 of the British Telecom PSS Users Forum (1980), *A Network Independent Transport Service* ('Yellow Book').

Study Group 3 of the British Telecom PSS Users Forum (1981), *Character Terminal Protocols on PSS* ('Green Book').

Wilkes, M. V., and Wheeler, D. J. (1979), *Proc. of Local Area Communications Networks Symposium*, NBS.

Glossary

ALOHA — A network operated by University of Hawaii using UHF packet broadcasting techniques.

Alphabet — An agreed character set used to represent data, for example, ASCII (q.v.).

AM — Amplitude Modulation, a type of modulation where the carrier (q.v.) is varied in its amplitude in sympathy with an information signal.

Analogue transmission — Transmission system in which the modulation of the carrier varies in exact sympathy with the information signal.

ARPA — Advanced Research Projects Agency of the US Department of Defense.

ARPANET — One of the first large scale packet switched networks linking academic institutes involved in ARPA work.

ASCII — American Standard Code for Information Interchange.

Audio frequency — Frequencies which fall within the range of hearing of the human ear, about 20 Hz to 20 KHz.

Bandwidth — Range of frequencies which a channel is capable of transmitting.

Baseband — The original frequency components of an information signal.

Baud — Unit of signalling speed, one signal element per second. Since a signal element can represent more than one bit it is not synonymous with bps.

BCC — Block Check Character, see LRC.

Bit — Contraction of 'binary digit'.

bps — Bits per second.

Buffer — Storage area for intermediate data, sometimes used to accommodate speed differences in data rate.

BT — British Telecom, the nationalised common carrier in the UK.

Byte — A group of bits used to define a single character. Often 8 bit bytes are used, also termed octet.

Carrier — A single frequency capable of being modulated by an information signal.

CCITT — The initials of the French name for the International Telegraph and Telephone Consultative Committee. Part of ITU (q.v.) in which representatives from national telecommunications networks agree on common standards for interworking.

Channel — A path along which a signal can be sent.

Common carrier — A US term for a company offering public communications services.

Concentrator — A device which accepts data from a number of lines and sends it down a single line; also receives data from the single line and sends it down the appropriate line.

Contention — Competition between different parts of a system for a limited resource.

Control character — A character in an alphabet reserved for some controlling purpose rather than for carrying data.

Data — Information represented in some formalised way, typically digitally for storage or processing.

Datagram — A packet sent independently of others in the network containing its destination address, compare virtual circuit.

Data Rate — The rate at which a channel can carry data, measured in bps.

Data Set — Alternative name for modem (q.v.).

DCE — Data Circuit Terminating Equipment. Term used to describe a network up to and including the modem to which the subscriber's equipment (DTE) is connected by a standard interface.

Demand multiplexing — A type of time division multiplexing in which the allocation of time-slots to each subchannel depends on the amount of data to be sent.

DTE — Data Terminal Equipment, the users equipment connected to a network.

Duplex circuit — A circuit which will permit transmission in both directions.

FDM — Frequency Division Multiplexing. A method of combining several analogue signals by modulating several carriers so they each fit into part of a spectrum of signals to be sent down a wide bandwidth channel.

Flag — In HDLC procedures the octet (01111110) is used to delimit the start and end of frames.

FM — Frequency Modulation. A type of modulation in which the frequency of the carrier is altered in sympathy with the information signal.

Full-duplex — A transmission channel which can carry signals in both directions simultaneously.

Gateway — A processor which connects two networks, appears to each network as a node.

FTP — File Transfer Protocol. A high level protocol.

Half-duplex — A transmission channel which can carry signals in either direction but not simultaneously.

HDLC — High-Level Data Link Control. A set of protocols defined by ISO for carrying data over a transmission channel embodying error control and flow control.

High-level protocol — A protocol which handles functions at a higher level than merely carrying data, for example, FTP.

Interface — A boundary, either in hardware or software across which the interaction of two processes is defined.

ISO — International Standards Organisation.

ITU — International Telecommunications Union, a UN body made up of CCIR (for radio communications) and CCITT.

JTMP — Job Transfer and Manipulation Protocol, a high-level protocol for remote job submission and control.

LAP — Link Access Procedure, the subset of HDLC specified for use as the link level in X.25 networks.

LAP-B — As LAP but specifying the 'balanced' HDLC option.

Leased line — A communications channel hired from a common carrier for the exclusive use of the subscriber between two or more fixed points.

LRC — Longitudinal Redundancy Check, an error detecting character sequence formed by taking the parity of each row of bits from 2^0 to 2^6 in a message.

Message — A block of data which the user wishes the communications network to carry as an indivisible entity.

Message switching — A mode of operating communications network in which the basic unit of transmission is the message.

Modem — Modulator-demodulator. A device which accepts a digital waveform and modulates a suitable carrier in order to transmit it over an analogue channel, also receives analogue signals from a distant modem and generates digital form.

Modulation — The process of altering some characteristic of a carrier wave in sympathy with an information signal.

Multidrop line — A leased line with several connections along its length.

Multiplexor — A device which splits a single high speed channel into several low speed channels, similar to a concentrator but generally implemented in hardware.

Node — A junction between two or more lines in a network. In a packet switched system it refers to a switching processor.

Octet — An 8 bit byte.

Packet — A block of data of limited size with a fixed header used to convey data through a packet switched network, a message might be sent as several packets.

Packet switching — A mode of network operation on which the basic unit of information transported between nodes is the packet.

PAD — Packet Assembler/Disassembler. A processor which converts between packets and a character stream suitable for simple terminals.

Parity — The property of being either odd or even. Often used in error detection, the number of binary ones in a character or message is counted and the total always made odd or even by the possible addition of an extra 'one'.

Permanent virtual circuit – A virtual circuit set up permanently by the operators of a packet switched network between two subscribers, analogous with
leased line.

Polling – A term used in protocols to invite the other end of a data link to
transmit data.

Protocol – A definition of what data and when may be sent across an interface.

PSS – Packet Switched Service. A packet switched national network operated
by British Telecom.

Queue – A buffer for messages or data whose access regime is 'first in, first out'.

Real time system – A computer system which must respond to outside events
within a limited time.

RJE – Remote Job Entry, submission over a data link or network of batch jobs
for execution by a computer system.

Semaphore – A concept introduced by Djikstra to synchronise processes. A
process may include a 'wait' for a semphore, if the semaphore is set when
the 'wait' is executed it continues processing, otherwise it waits until some
other process sets it.

Signal – The physical form of some information transfer may be voltage or
current waves, light in an optical fibre etc.

Store and forward – A mode of network operation in which each message is
placed on backing store before sending to the next node.

Tariff – The published rate charged by a common carrier for a particular facility.

TDM – Time Division Multiplexing. A method of sending several slow channels
down a single fast channel by dividing access to the fast channel into time
slots allocated cyclically to the slow channels.

Teletext – A system of data transmissions sent as part of the television signal for
reception on special domestic TVs.

Telex – The public circuit switched teleprinter network.

Time-out – A period of time agreed between two processes as the maximum
duration some process may take; it is assumed to have failed if it is exceeded.

Transparency – The property of a data link which enables any sequence of bits
to be sent through it and received without alteration, that is, there are no
reserved characters.

TS – Transport Service. A standard interface for processes using a network so
that they need not concern themselves with the formats of bit settings of
packets etc. but only see a stream of octets between two processes.

Virtual call – A virtual circuit set up at user request when it is needed and terminated when no longer needed, analogous with a dial-up line.

Virtual circuit – A facility in packet switched network in which packets sent
between two subscribers maintain their sequence.

V-series – Recommendations by the CCITT on the use of the telephone network
for data transmission, for example, V.24 for interface signals to medium
speed modems.

Wideband channel — A channel wider in bandwidth than a standard voice grade telephone channel.

X-series — CCITT recommendations for new data networks, for example, X.25 for packet switched networks.

Index

Index